Understanding English Homonyms

Understanding English Homonyms

Their Origins and Usage

Alexander Tulloch

HKU PRESS
香港大學出版社

Hong Kong University Press
The University of Hong Kong
Pokfulam Road
Hong Kong
www.hkupress.org

© 2017 Hong Kong University Press

ISBN 978-988-8390-63-2 (*Hardback*)
ISBN 978-988-8390-64-9 (*Paperback*)

British Library Cataloguing-in-Publication Data
A catalogue record for this book is available from the British Library.

10 9 8 7 6 5 4 3 2 1

Printed and bound by Hang Tai Printing Co., Ltd. in Hong Kong, China

Contents

Introduction

It may seem rather odd, but there is currently no book available (as far as the present author has been able to ascertain) which explains the derivation of the many homonyms we have in English. There are books, of course, which deal with this feature of the language, but they are for the most part little more than word lists. Curious readers who wish to understand why, for example, we can 'file' our fingernails but also 'file' documents away for safekeeping and easy future access have to work patiently through etymological dictionaries, perhaps including those written in foreign languages, in order to satisfy their curiosity. The aim of the present volume, therefore, is to draw together a few of the linguistic threads behind many of the homonyms in daily use among English speakers and to acquaint the reader with etymological explanations for their existence. Teachers, lecturers, linguists, writers, and native and foreign students of English will hopefully find the following pages compelling and informative.

The Definition

There is a problem, however, with the stated aim of this book, as there is no absolute definition of what a homonym is. The strictly traditional view is that a word can be defined as a homonym if it is spelled and pronounced the same as another but has a different meaning. If we consider, for instance, the sentence 'Is the still still still?' (i.e., 'Is the apparatus for producing alcohol as motionless as it previously was?'), we can safely say that all three 'stills' are spelled and pronounced exactly the same but have totally different meanings. They can therefore be classed as homonyms.

Unfortunately, some authorities include homophones (words pronounced the same but spelled differently, e.g., 'gait' and 'gate') under the banner of homonyms, and this has tended to complicate matters a little. Then there is the question of homographs, and here too dictionaries can differ in the definitions they offer the reader. Some infer that homographs and homonyms are virtually interchangeable terms; others define homographs as words which have the same spelling but totally different meanings and possibly pronunciations, such as the 'winds' that blow as opposed to the road that 'winds'. Against this background of apparent confusion, the working hypothesis adopted during the preparation of this book is that a homonym is a word which is simultaneously a homophone and a homograph.

This, however, is not quite the end of the problem as there is still the question of the distinction now made between *homonyms* and *polysemous homonyms*. The former group includes those words which are written alike, have totally different meanings, and are also descended from two distinct sources. The word 'bear' is a case in point. When it means 'to carry', it is allied to a reconstructed Indo-European root meaning both 'to carry' and 'to give birth'. On the other hand, when it denotes the dreaded beast of the forest, it is derived from a Germanic root meaning 'brown'.

Polysemous homonyms (i.e., homonyms with several meanings) occur where words have widely divergent usages but can be traced back to a common source. In such cases the explanation usually involves nothing more complicated than the passage of time and an imaginative manipulation of the language. A lady reading the latest edition of a fashion magazine and a soldier snapping the magazine into place on his rifle might not realize that the terms for the objects they are each holding in their hands share the same derivation, but they do. The original Arabic word, *makhzan*, meaning simply 'a store', made its way across the Mediterranean Sea centuries ago and has been adopted and adapted by several European languages to suit a variety of contexts. For the purposes of this book, no distinction has been made between the two types of homonym, as sufficient information is given under each headword for further comment to be redundant.

The Origins

The obvious question for anyone interested in the derivation of homonyms has to be: why does English have so many? The simplest answer is, of course, why not? English, like many or even most languages of the world, has been subjected to outside influences for centuries and ever-increasing contact with other societies introduced foreign words into these islands where they either coexisted with or replaced much of the native vocabulary.

Conquest brought the Romans, the Anglo-Saxons, the Danes, the Vikings, and the Normans to these shores. The Celtic ancient Britons, who had previously occupied the land, were pushed out to the edges of what became the British Isles, but they left traces of their languages in place names and a number of words which survive hidden away in everyday English, even if few people realize their provenance. In the world of religion, science, education, and the arts, words that had begun life in Latin, Greek, or Arabic also made their way into English. War, the scourge of Europe over the centuries, introduced words from all the nations we have fought against (and alongside) as our soldiers came into contact with their foreign counterparts on distant battlefields. Commerce, greater cultural contact, and Britain's expansionist colonial past meant that French, German,

Spanish, and Dutch words, as well as some from more exotic languages such as Russian, Hindi, Arabic, and Chinese, lodged themselves firmly in what we sometimes erroneously think of as *pure* English.

Nor should we forget the influence on the evolution of English homonyms exerted by the somewhat erratic development of a universally accepted system of spelling. In Chaucer's time, the orthography of the language was fairly chaotic. By Shakespeare's day a more stable complexion could be detected, but it was not until the eighteenth and nineteenth centuries, with the advent of dictionaries and more universal education, that genuine steps towards a standardized system of spelling became apparent.

Taking all these factors into consideration, it is hardly surprising that, metaphorically speaking, linguistic wires became crossed and meanings became confused to such an extent that written and spoken English was the unwitting victim. And in the midst of such a linguistic maelstrom, it should not come as a shock that the lexical combinations we refer to as 'homonyms' found their way into modern English.

Linguistic Prehistory

In 1786 the English orientalist Sir William Jones noticed that many words occurring in Latin, Greek, and Sanskrit bore a remarkable similarity, not only to each other but also to their English equivalents. In particular, the numerals and terms denoting family relationships in the different languages seemed to resemble each other far too closely for it to be the result of pure chance. He therefore put forward the theory that at some point in history there must have been a parent language from which subsequent ancient and modern languages of Europe and parts of Asia developed. Various terms for this parent language were proposed, but eventually linguists settled on Proto-Indo-European, although this is now frequently referred to simply as Indo-European.

Where and exactly when this archaic, unrecorded language existed nobody knows for certain; the generally accepted view is that it was possibly spoken somewhere in the region of eastern or central-eastern Europe as long ago as 3000 BC, but the theories concerning this parent language are based more on a mixture of educated deduction and speculation rather than hard evidence or fact. One leading French etymologist, Antoine Meillet (1866–1936), did go so far as to state that anyone wishing to hear what the original Indo-European language sounded like need do no more than engage a Lithuanian peasant in conversation. His studies had led him to the conclusion that modern Lithuanian preserves more of the original Indo-European sound system than any other living language.

If we consider the language map of the world today, however, there is little need for doubt or even discussion. Centuries of historical migrations from somewhere in the region of the Black Sea to all corners of the earth have ensured that the descendants of the postulated original Indo-European language (including English) are now more widely spoken throughout the world than those of any other language group.

When the early etymologists had gleaned all the data they could by analysing available texts written in Latin, Greek, and Sanskrit, they continued their research by what is now termed 'linguistic reconstruction'. They compared existing languages, sought patterns in sound shifts (i.e., observed how the vowels and consonants changed as words moved from one language to another), and attempted to establish what the historical form of a given word might have been. A good example of the method employed would be their examination of the modern English word 'lie' (as in 'assume a horizontal position') since it has clearly discernible relatives in the Latin and Greek words for 'bed', *lectus* and *lekhos,* the modern French *lit* and Spanish *lecho,* as well as the closely related Russian verb *lech'* ('to lie down'). By analysing these words and working backwards through history and linguistic change, etymologists have concluded that an original Indo-European form close to **legh* must have existed at one time. Such reconstructed forms are now, by convention, preceded in textbooks and dictionaries by an asterisk to indicate that they are unrecorded, and the practice has been adhered to throughout this volume. The same marker is also used in the case of words which should exist in otherwise well-attested languages, such as Old English and medieval Latin, but have not been documented.

The corpus of historical information now at the disposal of linguists means that they have a useful, if debatably theoretical, basis from which to work when attempting to understand the derivation of words in ancient and modern Indo-European languages. These reconstructed forms frequently proved an invaluable reference guide to the present author when selecting those homonyms with the most interesting histories for inclusion in this book.

Sound Shifts

One of the most important observations made by the nineteenth-century linguists was that certain consonants change in a more or less consistent pattern as they move from one language (or group of languages) to another. In essence this meant that, for instance, the sound represented by the letter 'p' in Greek and Latin frequently became an 'f' in the Germanic languages: *patēr, pater, father;* the sound represented by 'ph' or 'f' became a 'b' (*pherein, ferre, bear*). Under certain circumstances, a Greek 'p' could also become a 'b' in English, hence the correlation between the Greek *peithesthai,* Latin *fidere,* and Old English *bīdan* ('to trust'). The change from an unvoiced 'f' to its voiced equivalent 'v' is also seen in a comparison of the word *fan* and its Latin cognate verb, *ventilare* ('to fan').

Another change which the early etymologists identified was that from a Greek aspirate 'h' to a sibilant 's' in other European languages: *helios/sun, huios/ son, hals/salt.*

Under the headword WAGE readers might find that yet another consonant change (w–g) needs some clarification. The simplest explanation is that words of Germanic origin frequently altered an initial 'w' to a 'g' or 'gu' sound as they moved into French (and other Romance languages), thus: *wage/gagier*, *war/guerre*, *ward/garde*, and *wardrobe/garde-robe*.

Macrons

Macrons (i.e., diacritics indicating the lengthening of a vowel sound) have been preserved in words of Old English or Norse origin for the sake of consistency with reference works consulted during the preparation of this book.

In Greek words, the macrons indicate vowel lengthening as represented by different Greek letters. Hence the letter 'e' equates to the short epsilon (ε) and 'ē' to the long eta (η). The letter 'o' equates to the Greek short 'o' or omicron (o) and 'ō' to the Greek long 'o' or omega (ω).

Greek Transliteration

Readers should note that in Greek, the first 'g' in the combinations 'gg', 'gk', and 'gkh' is pronounced as an 'n'. Consequently, *aggelos* ('angel') and *aggelia* ('message') are pronounced *angelos* and *angelia* respectively.

The Letter Eth (ð)

Again, for the sake of consistency with other sources, the letter eth (ð) has been retained in words of Old English, Icelandic, and Old Norse origin. In modern English, eth equates to the combination 'th', pronounced as in both 'father' and 'thinner'.

Dates

Unless otherwise stated, the dates given in the following pages refer to the year, decade, or century for which there is written evidence of a given word. It is possible (or even highly probable) that many words existed in spoken form prior to being written down, but any attempt to specify the original date of oral usage would be little more than speculation.

ABIDE

Examples: (a) '**Abide** with Me' is a popular old hymn.

(b) 'I cannot **abide** that man!' she said, storming out.

a) The verb 'to abide' appeared in Old English as *ābīdan* or *gebīdan* ('to remain', 'to wait', or 'to dwell'). It is not very common in modern English as a synonym for 'to wait' and tends to survive mainly in a few set phrases. We still have expressions such as 'to abide by the law', 'an abiding memory', and a homeless person can be described (using the derivative noun) as being 'of no fixed abode'. A patient man, however, is said 'to bide his time', where 'to bide' is derived from another cognate Old English verb *bīdan* ('to await' or 'to dwell').

Linguists have had a considerable problem with the origin of this word. Some have suggested that the Indo-European root is **bheidh* ('to trust' or 'to persuade'), which would make the word cognate with Latin *fidere* ('to trust' or 'to persuade') and the Greek *peithesthai* ('to believe' or 'to trust in somebody'). There is possibly a connection here with the expression 'abiding by (i.e., trusting) the law', but it is difficult to see the connection between the Latin and Greek verbs on the one hand and concepts of dwelling or waiting on the other. One possible explanation is that 'waiting' and 'expecting' involve a belief or trust that someone or something will arrive sooner or later. There could be a parallel here with the idea of a lovers' tryst. The fourteenth-century word 'tryst' is cognate with the word 'trust' so that the man waiting for his lover might be said to be 'trusting' that she will appear.

b) The use of 'to abide' meaning 'to tolerate' is thought to be a colloquial deviation and was not recorded before the fifteenth century. On the other hand, it was a standard secondary meaning of the Old English *bīdan*, which would suggest that the link between 'waiting' and 'tolerating' has always been a close one.

It is interesting how this verb mirrors an almost identical additional use of the verb 'to stand'. Originally meaning 'to occupy a certain position', by the 1620s it was being used as a substitute for 'to tolerate' or 'to endure', and its use in such a context survives today.

ADDRESS

Examples: a) 'What is your **address**, sir?' asked the policeman.

b) The public **address** system was switched off.

a) The use of this word to designate a person's fixed abode has only been a feature of English since the nineteenth century. Its original meaning, dating from the early fourteenth century, was 'to guide' and was adopted into the language from Old French *adrecier*, which could mean (i) 'to go straight towards something', (ii) 'to set right', or (iii) 'to point to or direct somebody towards a certain place'.

Adrecier itself came from the vulgar Latin *addirectiare* (from the preposition *ad* ('to' or 'towards') and *directiare* ('to straighten')), linked to the Latin adjective *directus* ('straight') and the verb *dirigere* ('to straighten' or 'to direct').

The original meaning of 'address', therefore, was not so much the place where one lived but the means of getting there (i.e., in a straight line from another place). Its use on written communications is recorded from the fifteenth century, and the practice of writing it on the front of an envelope dates from around 1712.

Interestingly, the same Latin root produced another English verb, 'to direct', as well as its associated noun, 'direction'. This, in addition to the meaning we attach to it today, was historically the term for the name and address of the intended recipient as written at the beginning of a letter. This use of the word is echoed in the modern Spanish *dirección* ('address' or 'place of residence').

b) To 'address' somebody in the sense of speaking to them directly dates from the late fifteenth century and has given rise to a number of usages. It is now possible to 'address' a crowd or audience, and we commonly hear of a problem being 'addressed' (i.e., our attention is 'directed' at it) in the hope that a satisfactory solution will be found.

ARCH

Examples: a) They met by the clock underneath the big **arch**.

b) **Arch**duke Ferdinand was assassinated in 1914.

a) The architectural structure takes its name from the Latin *arcus* ('bow' or 'curve'), which has provided several related words both in English and other languages. 'Arcade', for instance, entered English from the Italian term *arcata*, a popular arched feature of the built environment in many European cities in the eighteenth and nineteenth centuries. Another derivative Latin word was *arca*, meaning a 'chest' or an 'ark' in which documents and valuables were kept hidden away from prying eyes. Consequently, anything contained within would be considered *arcanus* ('hidden', 'secret', or, as we now say, 'arcane'). And as *arcus* could additionally mean 'bow' (as in 'bow and arrow'), it is also the derivation of the sport we refer to as 'archery'. Strangely, however, this Latin word showed up in Gothic as *arhwazna* and later in Old English as *earh*, but by then the meaning in both languages had changed to 'arrow'. So when we talk about a 'bow and arrow' we are really just repeating ourselves.

b) 'Arch' as a prefix is derived from a totally different source, the Greek verb *arkhein* ('to rule' or 'to be the head of'). Consequently, we now have in English common words and expressions such as 'archbishop' (head bishop), 'archdeacon' (head deacon), 'archduke' (head duke), 'arch-enemy' (main enemy), and many more. The word 'architect', defining a highly qualified designer of buildings, is of rather humble linguistic origins. It comprises two Greek words, *arkhein* and *tektōn* ('builder' or 'carpenter'), so that the original meaning of the combined words was simply something along the lines of 'chief construction worker'. Furthermore, in historical times builders would have drawn up plans before they began work and deposited them for safekeeping in the *arkheion*, which in ancient Athens was the residence of the *arkhōn*, the chief magistrate. And *arkheion* gave us the word 'archive'.

But the verb *arkhein* had another meaning: 'to begin' or 'to be the first'. This explains why it also appears in English words not associated with the idea of ruling. 'Archaeology' is the study of the first stages of history; an 'archetype' is an original form or model; and 'archaic', now used to mean simply 'very old', was originally an adjective approximating to 'dating from the beginning'.

ATLAS

Examples: a) **Atlas** was one of the many Greek gods.

b) He took down the **atlas** and opened it at a map of France.

a) According to Greek mythology, Atlas was one of the older gods punished by Zeus for leading the Titans in a war against the Olympian gods. The form this punishment took was arduous: he was banished to the ends of the earth, to the garden of the Hesperides, and condemned to hold up the earth and sky for eternity.

The name Atlas is derived from the Greek infinitive *tlēnai* ('to bear' or 'to withstand'). Its Indo-European root is **tol/*tele*, frequently found in words associated with shoring up heavy weights or objects. It is cognate with the Latin *tolerare*, from which the English 'to tolerate' is derived, as well as the word 'talent'. In the monetary sense, a 'talent' was originally a coin that had been placed in a *talanton* (Greek for 'scales'), so that its weight and value could be assessed. A 'talent' in the sense of a special gift is derived from the belief that our abilities are weighed out in the scales of destiny and apportioned to us at birth.

b) The convention of referring to a book of maps as an 'atlas' dates back to 1585 when the first of its kind was published by Gerardus Mercator, whose real name was Gerhard de Kremer (1512–1594). He was a Dutch cartographer and teacher of mathematics who fell foul of the authorities because his views were considered somewhat heretical. When he published his first maps of the world, he came up with the idea of having an image of Atlas holding the earth on his shoulders as part of the design for the frontispiece. From then on, it became the custom for all such books to bear the image of Atlas until eventually they came to be known by the image of the hapless god rather than their contents.

The mountain in north-western Africa known as Mount Atlas also takes its name from the same god because it was seen as the pillar of heaven holding up the sky as Atlas had held up the world. And the waters surrounding the mountain (known in Greek as the *atlantikē thalassa* ('Atlas Sea')) took their name from the same source until around 1600 when the term was applied to the body of water we now know as the Atlantic Ocean.

ATTIC

Examples: a) The professor was renowned for his **Attic** wit.

b) They converted the **attic** into an extra bedroom.

a) 'Attic' (*attikos* in Greek) is an adjective meaning 'pertaining to Attica', the region of Greece which was ruled in antiquity from the city we now think of as the capital of the whole country, Athens. During the fourth and fifth centuries BC the city state, as it was then termed, saw a blossoming of learning and culture which can be said to have laid the foundation of modern Western culture. Philosophers (e.g., Socrates, Plato, and Aristotle), playwrights (e.g., Euripides, Sophocles, and Aristophanes), historians (e.g., Thucydides and Xenophon), and orators (e.g., Pericles and Demosthenes) all contributed to what we now think of as Greek learning. The expression now used in English, 'Attic wit' (and its alternative 'Attic salt'), is a reflection of the highly refined sense of irony and sarcasm frequently displayed by these exponents of Greek learning.

b) Also with roots in Greek culture is the room at the top of the house we refer to as the 'attic'. Until the eighteenth century the full term was 'attic room', but this usage has since fallen out of favour, with the result that what is essentially an adjective is now used as a noun.

In classical architecture, the 'attic' was not part of a building's interior at all but a reference to the external pilasters (columns which are merely there to add decoration to an edifice) above the entablature. It was not until the eighteenth century that the word was applied to the interior room situated in the uppermost part of a building immediately beneath the roof.

A common alternative to the attic is the garret. This noun is derived from the Old French *garir* ('to defend') and was originally a watchtower designed to be part of a building's defensive features. It survives also in the modern English word 'garrison' (a building in which troops are housed).

Since about 1300 the word 'loft' has served as yet another alternative for the upper room in a house. This is essentially the Old English *lyft* ('sky' or 'air') and is cognate with the German *Luft* ('air').

BACHELOR

Examples: a) He remained a **bachelor** until he was in his fifties.
b) He graduated as a **Bachelor** of Arts in English.

a) It was not until the fourteenth century that 'bachelor' was applied in English to young unmarried men. There is some conjecture as to the origin of the term, but linguistic authorities agree that there is a possible link with the medieval Latin *baccalaria*, an area of land on a small farm or estate; the associated noun, *baccalarius*, is known to have been a term for a male or female peasant employed by a tenant farmer in the eighth century. In the thirteenth century we find the term 'knights bachelor' applied to young men who still had to grow a few inches before being considered fully fledged knights.

b) In or around the fourteenth century, when universities began appearing on the scene, the term *bacheler* (as it was spelled in Old French) was applied not only to young unmarried men but more specifically to those young unmarried men who had gained the lowest level of university qualification.

Some etymologists, however, maintain that there is another reason why students who have gained their first degree are referred to as 'bachelors'. They point to a possible linguistic link here with the Latin *bacca lauri* ('laurel berry') and the custom of awarding such berries as a symbol of academic success. This theory is not as far-fetched as it might sound; laurel wreaths in ancient times were frequently awarded to outstanding poets, writers, and so on. The practice is enshrined in terms we still use today, such as 'Poet Laureate' and 'Nobel Laureate'. We are also reminded of it when warned against 'resting on our laurels'.

BALL

Examples: (a) She completely missed the **ball** and lost the match.
(b) 'You shall go to the **ball**,' said Cinderella's fairy godmother.

a) The origin of the word is almost certainly Germanic and first appeared in English in its present form in the thirteenth century. In Old English it is thought to have been **beal*, from the Old Norse *bollr*. The word can ultimately be traced back to the Indo-European **bhel* ('to inflate' or 'to blow'), the same root that has given us words such as 'balloon' and 'bellows'. An interesting additional piece of information here concerns the word 'polo'. The first recorded polo match in England took place in Aldershot in 1871, no doubt played by soldiers who brought the name of the game back from India. 'Polo' is simply the word in Balti (a language related to Tibetan spoken in the Indus Valley) for 'ball'.

An Italian noun, *palla*, derived from the Germanic **balluz*, had the diminutive form *pallotte* ('little balls'), used for secret voting in Venice in the sixteenth century. This is the derivation of our 'ballot'.

b) When Cinderella went to the ball it is safe to presume that she behaved in a more restrained manner than the origin of the word would suggest. The Greek word *ballizein*, from which it evolved, originally meant 'to throw one's legs about' or 'to jump about all over the place'. With the passage of time it came to suggest more controlled movement, although the energetic and physically demanding gyrations can still be seen in the kind of dancing defined by another derivative word, 'ballet'.

Interestingly, the Greek *ballizein* was itself derived from another verb, *ballein* ('to throw'), which shows up in a surprising number of modern words. A 'problem' (from *pro+ballein*) is something which has been 'thrown in front of us'; 'ballistics' is basically the science of throwing things; and the medical condition known as an 'embolism', characterized by a clot 'thrown into' a blood vessel, is from *en+ballein*'.

There is a fascinating linguistic parallel here. 'To throw something in front' rendered into Greek produced the English word 'problem', but the same concept translated into Latin gives *proiacere* (from *pro* ('in front') and *iacere* ('to throw')), whence we derive the word 'project'.

BANK

Examples: a) They sat on the river **bank** watching the boats sail by.
  b) Pete worked in a **bank** all his life.

a) As far as we know, this word did not exist in Old English but made its appearance suddenly around the year 1200. It is probably Scandinavian in origin, related to the Old Norse **banki* (or *bakki*) from the Proto-Germanic **bangkon* ('slope') and **bankiz* ('shelf'). In a manner similar to its cognate noun 'bench' (Old English *benc*) it referred to a man-made earthwork, originally defining nothing more than earth heaped up and fashioned into some form of primitive seat. It has also been suggested that the ultimate source of the word is the Indo-European root **bheg* ('to break') as a river's 'bank' is where the land 'breaks off' and the river begins. If this is the case, there is an interesting parallel with the Latin *ripa* ('river bank'), derived from the Greek *ereipein* ('to break off'). And *ripa* can be seen in other linguistic descendants: the Latin *ad ripam*, literally 'to the bank', gave us the verb 'to arrive', and a 'rival' was originally a person with whom we were prepared to fight in order to protect our section of the river bank.

b) Banks have only existed as the financial institutions we recognize today since the fourteenth century. The English term was borrowed from the Italian moneylenders in cities such as Venice and Florence who conducted their affairs from behind a *banca* or bench. (The French also borrowed the word but spelled it *banque*.)

The associated term 'bankrupt' has the suggested following derivation. The Italian *banca rotta*, the origin of the English term, literally means 'broken bench or table'. This is direct reference to the medieval custom of smashing up the tables of any moneylenders who, for one reason or another, failed in business and perhaps lost their clients' money. Presumably the idea was that if they had no bench from which to conduct their business they could no longer offer their services. This may also be why we talk of 'being broke' when we are in straitened financial circumstances.

BARK

Examples: a) They stripped the **bark** off the tree.
b) Poets sometimes call boats **barks** or barques.
c) All dogs **bark**.

a) The skin of a tree has been referred to as the 'bark' since around 1300. It is descended from the Old Norse *borkr* and a Proto-Germanic root **barkuz*. All authoritative etymological sources are of the opinion that the word is connected with the word 'birch', which in Old English was *berc* or *beorc*, from the Indo-European root *bhereg* ('to gleam' or 'to be bright'). It is cognate with the Gothic *bairhts* ('clear' or 'bright') and is probably so called because of its light appearance when compared with other trees.

The original Old English word for the outer skin of a tree was *rinde*, the derivation of the modern word 'rind'. This was also used in the context of fruit and vegetables from around 1400 but in modern English is restricted almost exclusively to cheese and bacon. The noun is allied to the verb 'to rend', from the Old English *hrendan* ('to tear off' or 'to cut down').

b) Although largely restricted in use to poetry now, the word 'bark' can still be applied to a little sailing vessel. It entered English in the fifteenth century from Middle French *barque*, borrowed from an unrecorded vulgar Latin **barica*. By the seventeenth century the term had acquired a more precise meaning of a three-masted ship. In modern English, of course, it survives in the expressions 'to embark' and 'to disembark'.

The word is closely connected with its cognate 'barge', from the medieval Latin *barca*, a word probably cognate with the Latin *baris* meaning an 'Egyptian boat'. The Greeks also used the word *baris* to define a certain kind of raft as well as the craft we would now refer to as a 'canoe'.

c) When we talk about a dog's bark (for which the Old English was *beorcan*) all we are doing really is imitating the sound. There appears to be no other etymological explanation.

BATTERY

Examples: a) They were both charged with assault and **battery**.
            b) During the war he served in an anti-aircraft **battery**.
            c) I must buy a new **battery** for my watch.

a) English acquired the word 'battery' in the sixteenth century from Old French *baterie* ('beating' or 'bashing'). This in turn had been absorbed into the language from the Latin verb *battuere*, which meant both 'to hit repeatedly' and 'to fight with swords'. What we have here is possibly a reflection of how military training was conducted in Roman times: wild slashing movements with shafts of wood in training but with swords in times of war. Either way, the word survives both in colloquial English 'to batter' as a synonym for 'to beat' and as part of the legal term 'assault and battery'. 'Assault' (from the Latin *ad+salire* ('to leap at')) is a term applied to threats of violence, and 'battery' to actual physical attack.

b) With the advent of artillery in the Middle Ages, a word had to be found for the new concepts of warfare. 'Battery' was now adopted to describe the actions of the artillerymen who rained cannonballs down on enemy installations, 'battering' them into submission. Fairly soon, however, the word was applied not to the hail of artillery fire but to the means of delivering it. More specifically, it was eventually applied to clearly defined groups of cannons each under the command of a single officer.

c) There is still some disagreement among linguists as to how the word 'battery' came to be applied to the little stores of electricity which play such an important role in modern society. The American statesman Benjamin Franklin is credited with the first use of the word in 1748; he might have seen the similarity between a group of cannons assembled in one unit and the groups of cells bound together to form a 'battery' for storing electricity. The other theory is that a 'battery' discharges electricity much in the same way as an artillery 'battery' discharges cannonballs.

BAY

Examples: a) The little boat sailed into the **bay**.
            b) The **bay** leaf is widely used in cooking.
            c) He found himself in the sick **bay** for a few days.
            d) The dogs began to **bay** at the sight of the fox.
            e) The **bay** stumbled and fell.

a) The English form of the word came from the Old French *baie*, which was a borrowing of the Spanish *bahía*. According to some linguists, however, the Spanish word was itself a borrowing from the Basque, *badia* ('bay').

b) The leaf which plays such an important role in the culinary life of so many countries takes its name from an Old French word *baie*. But this word has nothing to do with sea inlets; it is derived from the Latin *baca* ('berry'), a reference to the berries on the shrub's leaves. By the 1520s, the derivative noun 'bay' was applied to the whole shrub itself.

c) It is tempting to think of 'bay' (a coastal inlet) as being the same as the architectural feature as both describe recesses of a sort. But 'bay window', 'sick bay', etc., are terms derived from Medieval Latin *batare*, the Old French *baer*, and modern French *bayer* meaning 'to gape'. In other words, a 'bay', as part of a room is really little more than a 'gap' in a wall.

d) Almost certainly the 'baying' of dogs is simply a variant of the barking of dogs and possibly connected with the Old French *abaiier* ('to howl'). If this is the origin of the word, it has given us another expression, 'to be at bay' (i.e., to feel threatened or in a difficult situation). The reference here is to how a hunted animal must feel when surrounded by howling or 'baying' hounds.

e) 'Bay' as a term for a reddish-brown horse is a direct borrowing from Old French *bai* and the Latin *badius*, an adjective used to describe chestnut brown horses.

BEAR

Examples: a) The load was too heavy for the wall to **bear**.
b) The hunters trapped the **bear** in a large net.

a) One of the interesting points about this word is the way in which it is used in all the Germanic languages to mean both 'carry' and 'give birth'. The very word 'birth' is itself a cognate, as is the word 'born' and the dialect word for a child, 'bairn'. And even further afield, we find the Russian cognate words *bremya* ('burden') and its derivative adjective *beremennaya* ('pregnant').

The Indo-European root here is **bher*, which is also seen in Old English *beran*, Middle English *bēre*, and Gothic *bairan*. It also produced the Greek and Latin infinitives *pherein* and *ferre* 'to carry' which have given English such words as 'to transfer' (to carry across), 'to defer' (to put off), 'to prefer' (to bring to the front), phosphorus (bringer of light), and many more. Even the word 'fertile' is cognate, basically meaning 'able to bear' fruit, crops, etc.

In most contexts in English the word has been replaced by 'to carry', although it survives in many set expressions. We talk about a 'load-bearing' wall, the 'bearings' of an engine, and 'ball bearings', not to mention the figurative uses in expressions such as having 'a cross to bear' and 'to bear a grudge'.

b) The traditional name for the 'bear' in English folklore is 'Bruin', and the appellation 'Bruin the Bear' is tautological. 'Bruin', 'bear', and the adjective 'brown' are all cognates derived from the Indo-European root **bhere* ('bright' or 'brown'). The Old English term for the animal was *bera*, directly descended from the Proto-Germanic **beron* ('the brown one').

The word for a bear in Greek was *arktos* (Latin had *ursus*), also used by the Greeks to denote the constellation known as the Great Bear. As this was seen mainly in the northern hemisphere, *arktos* acquired a more general meaning of 'the north' and eventually came to define the earth's most northerly region, the Arctic.

But the history of words associated with 'bear' contains a curious twist. No descendant of the Greek *arktos* made its way into the Germanic languages (or if it did, it is now lost) because of a superstitious belief that the mere mention of the animal which was the scourge of the northern climes would be enough to make it appear. Consequently, alternative terms were used, such as 'the brown thing', in the hope that such a periphrastic reference would prevent its appearance.

A further point worth noting involves the Celtic languages. Irish Gaelic retains *béar*, cognate with the Germanic term, but Welsh has retained *arth*, cognate with the Greek *arktos*.

BLAZE

Examples: a) The house was on fire, and the **blaze** could be seen for
miles.

b) Her horse had an unusually large **blaze** on its forehead.

c) They were determined to **blaze** the leader's name abroad.

a) This word has some of the most surprising connections in terms of the historical development of English. It entered English meaning 'to burn vigorously' in about 1200 as a derivative of the Old English *blæse* ('torch' or 'lamp'). Its roots lie in the Proto-Germanic **blas* ('shining' or 'white') and the Indo-European **bhel* ('to shine', 'to flash', or 'to burn'). The same root also produced Old English *blæcan* ('to bleach' or 'to whiten') and the Proto-Germanic **blakaz* ('burned'). This in turn produced the word *blāc* ('white'), as well as, almost unbelievably, *blaec*, the modern English word 'black'! In other words, the modern English terms 'black' and 'to bleach' (i.e., to whiten) share a common ancestry.

b) The 'blaze' on a horse's head is derived from the same Indo-European root and is so called because it is white and probably shiny. A surprising cognate adjective here, however, is 'bald'. This now always implies a lack of hair, but the original meaning of this adjective was 'white'. Evidence of this survives in the bird of prey known as the 'bald eagle'. It is certainly not 'bald' but more often than not flaunts a luxuriant display of glistening white plumage.

'Blazing a trail' is a reference to the pioneers in eighteenth century America who would hack their way through a forest and strip the bark off a tree or leave a white mark on the trunk to indicate to those following on behind which route they should follow.

c) The now somewhat archaic use of the word to mean making something public is derived from the Indo-European **bhle/*bhel* ('to blow' or 'to inflate'). It dates from a fourteenth century use of the word associated with blowing a trumpet and making people sit up and take notice whether they wanted to or not.

As a postscript, it is worth mentioning that the jacket known as a 'blazer' owes its origins to Cambridge University. In 1880, members of the Lady Margaret Boat Club (attached to St. John's College) took to wearing bright red jackets which soon became known as 'blazers' because of their conspicuously eye-catching appearance. Within a relatively short time, the name was applied to any similarly styled jacket, even if its colour was more muted.

BOX

Examples: a) She kept all his letters in a special little pink **box**.
            b) He learned to **box** when he was a schoolboy.

a) The receptacle which we generally refer to as a 'box' takes its name from the tree of the same name. It was already known in Old English as *box* and had been borrowed from the Latin *buxus*, which in turn was derived from the Greek *puxos* and its related adjective *puknos* ('thick' or 'dense'). In the world of horticulture, the box tree is known as possibly the hardest and densest of all European trees (it does not float in water), but it has another feature which makes it ideal for furniture making: it has almost no perceptible grain caused by growth rings. Obviously this feature was recognized in ancient times as it made its wood very easy to work with and the receptacles made from such a hard material would have been considered very secure.

In Britain the day after Christmas Day (i.e., 26 December) is known as Boxing Day, and for an explanation of the term we have to go back to the first half of the nineteenth century. The term is first attested in 1830 when little gifts were given to people such as postmen and delivery boys who had performed valuable service throughout the year. The expression 'Christmas Box', however, is much older and is a possible reference to the practice of handing out boxes of food and other goodies to the parish poor in the Middle Ages.

b) Boxing as a sport has been known since ancient times, and the expression 'to give somebody a box on the ears' was in common use in the time of Chaucer (1343–1400). It almost certainly entered English from Latin *pugnus* ('fist') and *pugnare* ('to fight'), the derivation of the adjective 'pugnacious'. The Latin terms appear to be cognate with the Greek adverb *pux* ('with clenched fist'), the noun *puktēs* ('boxer'), and the adjectival phrase *pux agathos* ('good with his fists'). The Latin and Greek words can all be traced back to the Indo-European root **puek/*peug* ('to stab' or 'to prod').

BROOK

Examples: a) His children liked to play in the little **brook** near their house.
            b) He is a stern master who will **brook** no impertinence.

a) In English it is conventional to talk about a 'babbling (i.e., gently murmuring) brook', and this disguises somewhat the etymology of the word. It is, in fact, closely related to the word 'break' and refers to a stream of water that bursts out through the earth. On the other hand, in some English dialects (and modern German which has *Bruch*) the word means 'bog' or 'marshland'. There is a link, however, in that the German *Bruch* also means a 'break'.

b) The use of the word to mean 'to tolerate' or 'to endure' is totally divorced from any associations with gently flowing rivers or marshland. The word's immediate antecedent is the Old English *brūcan* which could mean 'to use', 'to derive pleasure from', 'to possess', 'to eat', or even 'to cohabit with'. A close cognate is the modern German *brauchen* ('to need' or 'to use').

The word *brūcan* ('to derive pleasure from') was replaced in the late fourteenth century by the word 'to enjoy', derived from the Latin *en* ('in') and *gaudere* ('to rejoice').

The Indo-European root of *brūcan* is **bhreug* ('to use' or 'to enjoy') which is also the root from which the Latin *frui* ('to feed oneself' or 'to enjoy') is derived. The noun associated with this Latin verb was *frux* (genitive *frugis*), the source of the modern English 'fruit'. Etymologically speaking, therefore, 'fruit' was originally simply 'something that could be enjoyed'.

In archaic English 'to brook' in the sense of 'to put up with' is almost exclusively used with a negative meaning, as in, for example, 'she brooks no nonsense'.

BULL

Examples: a) The farmer led the old **bull** to market.

b) Papal **bulls** are issued by the Pope.

c) 'That's a load of **bull**!' said the policeman.

a) Old English and Old Norse had *bula* and *boli* respectively for 'bull', descended from the Proto-Germanic root **bullon* ('to roar'). In Old English there was also the related verb *bellan* ('to roar' but also 'to make a loud noise', hence the cognate noun 'bell'). Another, perhaps unsuspected cognate noun in English is 'boulder', a borrowing from the Swedish *bullersten*. This was a combination of *buller* ('to roar') and *sten* ('stone') and referred to the large stones in the middle of a fast-flowing river which produced a 'roaring' noise as the water washed over them. Other related words include 'bulldog', which from about 1500 was a description for dogs used in bull-baiting, and 'bulldoze', which originally meant 'to administer a dose big enough for a bull'.

b) The solemn edicts issued from the Vatican have been knows as papal bulls since around 1300. In medieval Latin a *bulla* was a sealed document, but originally the *bulla* was the seal itself. This was derived from the Latin *bulla* ('round swelling', 'bubble', or 'boss').

A variant of the term, 'bulletin' appeared in the eighteenth century as a borrowing from the Italian *bulletino*, a brief document containing information about foreign wars, affairs, etc.

c) 'Bull' meaning 'rubbish', 'nonsense', or 'not to be believed' is usually taken to be an abbreviation of 'bullshit' (i.e., totally worthless and unpleasant). But in fact this usage dates only from around the time of the First World War; the term itself was in use much earlier. It appeared in English in the seventeenth century as a description of statements not worthy of credence and is possibly connected with the Old French *bole* meaning 'deception' or 'trick'. Another possible connection is the sixteenth-century English verb 'to bull' meaning 'to mock' or 'to cheat'.

BUTT

Examples: a) All his arrows missed the **butt**.

b) There was only one **butt** of sherry left in the cellar.

c) Boxers are not permitted to **butt** their opponents.

a) Most etymologists seem to agree that there is an association between the French words *butte* ('a knoll'; surviving in the district of Paris known as *la Butte de Montmartre*) and *but* ('mark' or 'something to aim at'). The probability is that in its earliest sense a 'butt' was an embankment of sorts on which a target was placed and then shot at by archers. The use of the word in English to define the target itself dates from the fourteenth century.

b) This is not a word we use every day in English, but we do use several of its derivatives without even realizing the connection. In the late fourteenth century the word *butt* was being used in England to denote a cask of wine, beer, etc. This was derived from the Old French *bot* meaning 'wineskin' or 'barrel', from the late Latin *buttis* ('cask'). Another linguistic relative was the Old French *boteille*, from the vulgar Latin *butticula*, which also gave us the word 'bottle'. In modern English we also use the words 'butler' (strictly speaking, the man who is in charge of the bottles) and 'buttery', the correct term for the place where the 'butts' of wine, etc., are stored.

c) To strike, or 'butt', someone with the head also has some interesting relatives in modern English. In Old French *boter* meant 'to push' or 'to shove', a descendant from the Proto-Germanic root **butan* ('to strike'). The same root also produced 'bud' and 'button', which are both associated with the act of 'pushing' or 'thrusting' through.

There is an interesting comparison here with Greek, which had *eriphos* ('young goat'), cognate with the Latin *arietare* ('to butt') and its associated noun *airēs* ('a ram'). In its more usual form this is, of course, Aries, the ram of the zodiac.

There are several other usages linked with this word: since 1300 it has defined a kind of stubby flatfish; since 1400 it has been used for the 'thick end' of objects such as tree stumps; since the fifteenth century it has also denoted one's posterior. It was first applied to the remaining part of a cigar or cigarette in the nineteenth century.

CAMERA

Examples: a) The photographer bought himself a new **camera**.
b) The judge decided to hear the case in **camera**.

a) The ancient Greek verb *kamptein* meant 'to bend', and it gave rise to several surprising linguistic descendants. Its associated noun, *kamara*, basically meant 'curve' but came to be applied to almost anything with a curved or vaulted top. A carriage with a curved roof could be a *kamara*, as could a building with a vaulted arch. In the eighteenth century the phrase *camera obscura* appeared as an architectural term for a darkened, vaulted room, and so in the early days of photography, when a name was needed for the new device designed to capture images, the 'dark room' provided a perfect analogy. Now, of course, the device is known simply as a 'camera'.

b) The Greek noun *kamara* found its way into French and is the basis of the word we now recognize as *chambre*, or, in its English form, 'chamber'.

The legal profession in Britain has adopted the anglicized spelling of the word but has preserved the original French meaning. Barristers refer to their offices or rooms as 'chambers', and certain gentlemen of the legal profession refer to themselves individually as 'chamber counsel' meaning that they restrict themselves to offering advice in the privacy of their own chambers but do not defend clients in court. And judges, as and when they deem it appropriate to hear cases away from public scrutiny, do so 'in camera'. This is simply a legalese way of saying that the proceedings should be discussed in the privacy of the judge's 'chambers', or rooms.

Another surprising linguistic relative is the word 'comrade'. This now has certain political (particularly left-wing) overtones, but it entered French as *camarade* in the sixteenth century and was simply a term for somebody with whom one shared a room. A 'room-mate' would be nearest modern expression.

CANON

Examples: a) The **canon** asked the bishop to pass the port.
b) Shakespeare comes first in the **canon** of English literature.

a) The word *kanna* 'reed' or 'cane' was the name the ancient Greeks gave to the plant which grew so straight that it spawned a host of other words associated literally and metaphorically with ideas of correctness and the rule of law. A derivative noun in Greek was *kanōn*, which could refer to anything from a straight rod or bar to a carpenter's rule and this soon led to the figurative concept of a benchmark against which anything or anyone could be judged. In the plural, *hoi kanones* ('the models') were the writers of classical Athens who set the standard of excellence to which other writers were expected to aspire.

A 'canon' as a holder of clerical office was known in Middle English as a *canun*, a term derived from the Old French *canoine*, which in turn was derived ultimately from the Latin *canonicus* ('one who is subject to rule or law').

b) Historically, the term 'canon' was applied to a body of books approved by the Church, but by the mid-eighteenth century it had been secularized and designated almost any collection of works by a given author or on a given subject. Another theological use of the word is found in the related verb 'to canonize' (i.e., to include someone in the approved list of saints).

The homophone 'cannon' is a close linguistic relative. The Greek *kanna*, which provided a metaphorical gauge of rectitude or probity etc., also provided the term for the weapon of war which made its appearance in the Middle Ages. It was borrowed from the Italian *cannone*, also derived from the Greek *kanna*, because it was very straight like a reed, if perhaps a lot longer.

Other cognates include 'canal' and 'channel', which were both originally pipes (or perhaps even the reeds themselves) used for transferring water from one place to another.

CAPITAL

Examples: a) All countries have a **capital** city.

b) He has no income and is now living on his **capital**.

a) The word 'capital' is directly descended from the Latin *capitalis*, an adjective formed from the noun *caput* ('head'). There are many other words in English which, although not in immediately recognizable forms, have come down to us from this one Latin word. A 'chapter', for instance, is either a 'heading' for a section of a book or it can designate the governing body of a cathedral, usually consisting of canons and presided over by a dean. The 'capital' letters used at the beginning of a sentence or at the beginning of a name, indicate that they are the most important letters (i.e., at the 'head') of a word or sentence. And the idea of being in a position of authority is preserved in other derivative words: 'chef' (the head cook), 'chief' (the boss), etc.

But there are also other words in English and other languages which, perhaps surprisingly, are directly related to the Latin *caput*: to 'capitulate' was originally to surrender to a set of conditions listed under separate 'headings'; a 'cappuccino' coffee is one with a frothy 'head' and the order of Franciscan friars known as the Capuchins were so called because of their custom of covering their heads with a hood (*cappuccio* in Italian).

b) In the world of finance, of course, capital refers to monetary wealth; a man's capital is the main, or 'chief', part of his assets. His incomings and outgoings, his debts and savings are considered subsidiary.

CASE

Examples: a) 'In that **case**,' she said, 'I'm going to London.'

b) All his toys were kept in a little leather **case**.

c) The subject of a verb is always in the nominative **case**.

d) The notice was written in large, upper-**case** letters.

a) The use of 'case' to mean an event or occasion is a borrowing into English from Old French *cas*, which in turn is derived from the Latin *casus* ('chance', 'occasion', or 'mishap'). The verb from which this noun is derived is *cadere* ('to fall') as the basic idea behind its use is exactly the same as that seen in the archaic English 'to befall'. An expression such as 'whatever the case' is another way of saying 'whatever befalls' or, in more modern English, 'whatever happens'.

b) Early in the fourteenth century English acquired 'case' meaning 'a receptacle' from the Old French *casse*. This had found its way into French from Latin, which had *capsa* ('box'), a derivative noun from the verb *capere* ('to take hold of'). As many of these little boxes would have been used to store money, the word was soon applied to the contents of the boxes and developed in English into the word 'cash'.

c) Anyone who studies an inflected language such as Latin or Greek or, in the modern world, German or Russian, soon has to familiarize himself or herself with 'cases'. This was a concept devised by grammarians in the fourteenth century to define the roles and functions played by nouns, pronouns, and adjectives in a sentence. The term, once again, is from the Latin *casus* ('a falling away') as the nominative was considered the most important, and the other cases (vocative, accusative, genitive, dative, and ablative) were seen as 'falling away' in terms of importance or frequency of use.

d) 'Upper-case' and 'lower-case' letters were originally typesetters' terms and date from the very early days of printing—i.e., around the 1580s. The custom in those days was to keep all the individual letters (or 'types') in separate little boxes (or 'cases'), one above the other. The top one (i.e., the 'upper case') was reserved for the capital letters and the bottom one (i.e., the 'lower case') was for the small letters. Hence the printer would use 'upper-case' or 'lower-case' letters as and when required.

CHAP

Examples: a) The cold, wet weather had given him **chapped** legs.
            b) He was thought of as being quite a decent **chap**.
            c) In westerns the cowboys all wear **chaps**.

a) The painful sores, characterized by splitting and redness, which can affect the skin in the winter are generally referred to as 'chaps'. They take their name from the Middle English *chappen* ('to split' or 'to burst open') although the term's dermatological connotations apparently only entered English in the fourteenth century. The verb is directly related to the Old French *coper* ('to cut'; *couper* in modern French).

b) It is no longer a very common way of referring to a man, but 'chap' still survives in rather dated expressions such as 'a good chap', 'a decent chap', etc. The word itself is an abbreviation of 'chapman', which was originally a term for a tradesman or hawker of wares. It is derived from the Old English *ceapman*, the first element of which, *ceap*, meant 'a bargain' or 'commercial transaction'. The term survives in many English place names (often in slightly altered forms) and always designates what is or was once a market (e.g., Cheapside, Chipping Norton, Chipping Camden, or, as in the Lancashire village, simply Chipping).

The expression 'to chop and change', which now suggests vacillation and indecision, was a fifteenth-century expression meaning 'to bargain'. Presumably, commercial transactions always involved a certain amount of hesitation before a decision was made or an agreement reached, and this uncertainty has provided us with the modern meaning.

c) Aficionados of American western films will be acquainted with the leather or sheepskin protective leggings known as 'chaps' which cowboys wear over their trousers. This is an abbreviated form of the Spanish *chaparreras*, the leather leggings designed to protect the wearers from the *chaparral*, a kind of prickly thicket or undergrowth. But the variety of tree that lends its name to this kind of thicket (the *chaparro* or kermes oak) is native to countries surrounding the Mediterranean, so it appears that the Spanish conquistadores took the word *chaparreras* with them to the Americas in the sixteenth century. The ultimate etymological source is the Basque word *txapar* ('little thicket' or 'kermes oak').

CHARGE

Examples: a) He forgot to **charge** his phone.

b) How much did they **charge** you for that?

c) The general ordered a cavalry **charge**.

d) In court he faced a **charge** of murder.

a) For the original meaning of the word charge, we have to go back to ancient Rome and its principal mode of transport, the *carrus*, a kind of two-wheeled wagon. This noun gave rise to the late Latin verb *carricare*, which meant 'to load' a wagon or cart before taking it to its destination. By the thirteenth century the Latin terms had made their way into Old French which now had the verb *chargier*, still with the basic idea of 'loading'. The first use of it in an electrical context is thought to have been in the mid-eighteenth century, which saw the first experiments with electricity and attempts at its storage.

b) By the mid-fifteenth century the idea of loading or imposing a burden had acquired a more metaphorical sense, and 'to charge somebody' meant 'to impose a burden of expense' and then, more generally, 'to demand payment' for goods or services rendered.

c) The word's association with military activity is a little more difficult to explain. One suggestion is that the original idea was that soldiers would load their quivers with arrows or, later, muskets with powder and shot before preparing to do battle. At some point in history the meaning shifted to include running headlong at the enemy.

d) It is thought to have first entered legal terminology in the fourteenth century, when it was used as a term for court orders and injunctions. By the late fifteenth century it was used to mean a specific accusation.

There are two further surprising linguistic associations with the original Latin. The word 'cargo' is so common in English now that few people are probably aware that it is a foreign word, but it entered English from Spanish which has it as the normal word for 'load'. The other surprise is 'caricature'. This came into English from the Italian *caricare*, which originally meant simply 'to load' but acquired the more figurative meaning of 'overloading' or 'exaggerating', and a 'caricature' is, by definition, a grotesque exaggeration or 'overloading' of a person's prominent features.

CLIP

Examples: a) She couldn't find a paper **clip** for all her papers.
           b) He left his nail **clippers** in the hotel.
           c) She gave the boy a **clip** on the ear.

a) The 'clip' used for holding things together has a history dating back to the sexual goings-on in Saxon and medieval England. In Old English the verb *clyppan* meant 'to embrace' and by extension 'to love'. The Middle English related verb *clippen* meant 'to fondle', and this and the Old English form of the verb were both related to the Old Norse *klypa* ('to pinch' or 'to squeeze'). Probably the Old Norse is closest to the meaning we now associate with the act of 'clipping' papers or documents together.

b) 'To clip' meaning 'to cut' dates from the twelfth century and seems to be associated with the idea of 'pressing' things together. The reasoning here is that cutting hair, nails, etc., with an instrument designed for the purpose involves 'pressing' two blades together firmly and rapidly in order to snip off little bits at a time. The combination of speed and sharpness led to another meaning of the word: 'clipper' (a ship with a sharp bow built for rapid movement through the water).

An alternative suggestion is that the word has come down to us from a similar Old Norse word, *klippa*, and is simply imitative of the sound heard when something is being cut.

c) In the not too dim and distant past, when corporal punishment was considered quite normal, children were often disciplined by a 'clip around the ear'. Various explanations have been suggested for this expression, one of which is that 'clip' here is derived from the Latin and Greek *colaphus* and *kolaphos* respectively, both of which meant 'a swift blow with the hand'. If this is correct, there is another interesting linguistic connection; *colaphus* is related to the Latin *culpa* ('blame'), and in the Middle Ages an accused would be described in court as *culpable: prit d'averrer* ('guilty; [the prosecution] is ready to prove'). This was often abbreviated in documents to *cul. prit*, the source of the modern English 'culprit'.

COACH

Examples: (a) The **coach** skidded off the road because of the ice and snow.

(b) The football **coach** was pleased at how the team played.

a) The word 'coach' is one of very few which have entered English, as well as many other European languages, from Hungarian (others include *paprika, sabre, hussar,* and *shako*). History tells us that in the fifteenth century in the village of Kocs ('cs' in Hungarian is pronounced 'ch' as in 'church'), just under fifty miles west of Budapest, a certain peasant family made their living by making particularly fine wagons or carriages, renowned throughout the land for the skill and workmanship that went into their construction. Someone in the family even came up with the idea of incorporating springs into their design which gave travellers a much smoother ride. Such a carriage was known as a *kocsi széker* (literally, 'a carriage from Kocs'), but eventually the expression was abbreviated to many and various forms of *kocs* as it spread across Europe. German has *Kutsche*, Italian has *cocchio*. Spanish also has *coche*, which was the historical term for carriage but now is the normal word for a car or automobile.

b) By the time the word reached England not only had it become a term for a mode of conveyance but was also applied figuratively to teachers and tutors preparing students for examinations. By 1830 Oxford University was applying the term to tutors tasked with figuratively conveying students along the road to what everybody hoped would be a successful conclusion of their studies. A few years later, probably around 1860, a 'coach' was also a man or woman who instructed athletes in their chosen sport. There is a parallel here, of course, with the word 'train'. It too can either be a mode of transport or a verb suggesting preparation for a demanding test at some time in the future.

COPPER

Examples: a) Modern houses now have **copper** pipes for the plumbing.

b) The **copper** suddenly appeared and caught the thief.

a) When the Romans ruled most of the known world, they made great use of metals of all kinds. One of these metals they termed *aes* (ultimately the origin of the word 'ore'), which is variously translated in dictionaries as 'bronze', 'brass', or 'copper'. Strictly speaking, however, the only *aes* which should be referred to as 'copper' is that which was mined on the Mediterranean island of Cyprus.

The Romans used the island as a source of the metal they termed *aes cyprium* ('bronze, brass, or copper from Cyprus'). The Greeks referred to the island as Kupros, a name which they associated with the goddess of love, Kupris (an alternative name for Aphrodite), who was worshipped with particular fervour on the island and according to legend was born there.

Interestingly, in Roman times the word *aes* was also used to denote 'cash', 'money', or 'wages' much in the same way that small denomination coins in Britain are referred to as 'coppers'.

b) The use of the word 'copper' to denote a policeman almost certainly has its origins among the denizens of the criminal underworld in Victorian London. Alongside terms such as 'Peeler' and 'Bobby' (both taken from Sir Robert Peel, the prime minister who first set up a regular constabulary in nineteenth-century London), a 'copper' was understood as a uniformed representative of the law who had the authority to 'cop' miscreants. This word was a variant of the Old French *caper* ('to capture') and was itself derived from the Latin *capere* ('to seize').

The first usage of the word 'copper' for policeman is given as 1846.

CORN

Examples: a) The **corn** field looked beautiful against the setting sun.

b) She had a very painful **corn** on her little toe.

a) The word 'corn' exists in one form or another in all the Germanic languages; Old English and Middle English had *corn*, Old Norse had *korn*, modern German has *Korn*, and they are all descended from the Indo-European root **grno/*geren* and the Germanic root **kurnam*. Interestingly, the Indo-European root has several apparently disparate meanings: 'to grind', 'to mature', and 'to crumble with age'. This explains why there is a direct connection between words such as 'corn', 'grain', and even the Greek *gerōn* ('old man') and *graus* ('old woman'). The ancient Greeks must have spotted the similarity between a grain of corn, which can be ground down, and a man or woman of advanced years crumbling away with the passage of time. In Anglo-Saxon England the word *corn* had a diminutive form *cyrnel* ('little grain') which eventually produced the modern English 'kernel'. There is a further etymological connection here with the Latin *granum* (also from **grno* and cognate with 'grain'), meaning 'seed' or 'kernel', and a number of seeds set out in a line reminded the Romans of the arrangement of fibres inside a tree, which is why we talk of wood as having a 'grain'.

b) 'Corn' as a hard piece of skin is closely allied to the word 'horn'. They both come from the Indo-European root **ker* ('horn' or 'head') and are cognate with the Greek *keras* ('horn'). The cognate Latin word *cornu*, also meaning 'horn', had several additional meanings, including 'the end of a promontory' and 'the extremity of a country'. And this is directly linked to the county of Cornwall in the far south-west of England. The natives still refer to their part of Britain as *Kernow*, from the Celtic word *kernou* ('horn'), a direct borrowing of the Latin word *cornu*.

The alternative term for a 'corn' in English is a 'callus'. This entered English in the sixteenth century and is derived from the Latin *callere* ('to be hard').

COUNT

Examples: a) Toby sat on the bed and began to **count** his money.

b) The **Count** of Monte Cristo is a famous French novel.

a) In Old French the verb *conter* had two meanings, 'to add up' or 'to tell a story', and both meanings have remained very close to the way the word is used in modern English. We can 'count' money or instruct our 'accountant' to do it for us, but we can also give an 'account' of an incident we might have seen on the way to the shops. The equivalent verbs in other languages also show a remarkable similarity: modern French has *conter* ('to narrate') and *compter* ('to count'), German has *zählen* ('to count') and *erzählen* ('to narrate'), and Spanish has *contar* for both.

The original Latin verb from which the English, French, and Spanish verbs are derived was *computare* (which gave us the word 'computer'), a combination of *com* ('together' or 'with') and *putare*, a verb with several meanings including 'to reckon' and 'to estimate'. The basic idea of assembling information (numerical or factual) and presenting 'an account' explains the similarity of meaning that has survived to the present day.

b) When the Normans arrived in England in 1066 they brought their own system of government, and this frequently involved replacing Anglo-Saxon social-administration terminology with their own. One of the terms which they did not impose on the English, however, was *conte*, an Old French title translated into English as 'count'. The Anglo-Saxon equivalent was *eorl* (recognizable in modern English as 'earl') and the invaders allowed their new subjects to retain the term. Illogically, however, the wife of an English earl is a 'countess', and the areas of administration known as 'shires' before the Normans arrived acquired the alternative designation 'counties'.

The Old French term *conte* was derived from the Latin *comes* (genitive *comitis*), strictly an 'attendant' but in ancient Rome was also the term for a 'provincial governor'. *Comes* was derived from *cum* ('with') and *ire* ('to go'), so that the derivative compound noun originally meant 'a companion on a journey' or 'fellow traveller'.

CROSS

Examples: a) There was a huge wooden **cross** at the church door.

b) He could tell from her face that she was **cross** with him.

a) The original Old English word *rōd*, or 'rood' (derived from the Indo-European root **ret* ('post')), was the term in Saxon England for a cross, gallows, or simply a tall pole. In the mid-tenth century the Old Irish *cros* (derived from the Latin *crux*, although it has been suggested that the ultimate source is possibly Phoenician) made its way into English. Modern cognates include the French *croix*, Spanish *cruz*, German *Kreuz*, and Russian *krest*.

It is interesting to note the parallel between the Greek word *stauros*, usually translated as 'cross', and the Old English *rōd*. The basic meaning of both was a sharp stick or pole stuck in the ground. But when the Greek noun was made plural (*stauroi*) the resulting additional meaning was 'a palisade'. Palisades would frequently be used for protecting valuable goods such as food or weapons in a specific location, which came to be defined as a *staurōma*, and *staurōma* arguably evolved into Old French *estore*, which by the thirteenth century had entered English as 'store'. From the seventeenth century the word was used to denote a 'warehouse', and by the eighteenth it had acquired the meaning we attach to it today, 'a large shop'.

b) By the year 1200 the verb 'to cross' meaning 'to make the sign of the cross' had appeared in English, and then by about 1400 the same verb had come to define almost any motion from side to side. In a maritime sense, any wind that 'crossed' the direction of travel and adversely affected a ship's progress was considered unfavourable. This, it has been suggested, caused the sailors to feel angry and annoyed (in other words, it made them 'cross'), and this association with peevishness and bad temper has been dated to the 1630s. Another possibility, of course, is that it is linked to the aggressive attitude adopted by those prepared to 'cross' swords.

The maritime connection had a further development. The cognate Dutch verb *kruisen* ('to cross') appeared in seventeenth-century English as 'to cruise' with more or less the same meaning we attach to it today. Cruise liners, by definition, spend most of their time 'crossing' the world's seas and oceans.

CURRY

Examples: a) He was very partial to a good **curry** and a couple of beers.
           b) He was not the type to **curry** favour with anyone.

a) Since the 1960s there has been an enormous expansion of restaurants in the United Kingdom offering different kinds of cuisine from all over the world. As a result, our eating habits have changed considerably and delicacies such as the roast beef of old England, and traditional fish and chips have fallen down the league tables considerably.

The word 'curry' is one of a whole batch which entered English from the Indian subcontinent, partly as a result of the British Raj and partly as a result of immigrants from that part of the world who introduced many of their own customs to Britain. The original *kari* is simply 'sauce' in Tamil, a Dravidian language spoken in southern India and Sri Lanka.

b) 'To curry favour' is an expression of a very different sort and entered English through a rather circuitous route. The origins of the word 'curry' here are connected to an unattested vulgar Latin **conredare* ('to arrange' or 'to equip') and the Germanic **garaethjan* ('to prepare a horse for riding'). This is also cognate with the modern English 'ready', originally an adjective simply meaning that a horse was saddled and waiting to be taken out onto the open road.

By the thirteenth century the Old French verb *correier* ('to arrange' or 'to equip') had become 'curry' in English with the meaning of 'to rub down' or 'to brush'. By the fifteenth century, it had the more specific meaning of 'to dress leather' (i.e., to buff a hide until it is transformed into a soft, shiny material suitable for the manufacture of clothing or footwear). And *favel*, an Old French word for a chestnut-coloured horse, was replaced by 'favour' simply because it was more familiar to English ears. At some point, the action of brushing a horse acquired the metaphorical meaning of caressing somebody verbally in order to win favour.

The original equestrian connection explains why, as anyone familiar with horses knows, an indispensable implement found in any stable is the 'curry comb'.

DATE

Examples: a) She was quite excited about going on her first **date**.
       b) He ate the grapes but pushed the **date** to one side.

a) Since the fourteenth century the basic idea behind the word 'date', as used in English for a fixed appointment or specific day on the calendar, has been that it defines a 'given' point in time. The immediate linguistic root is the Latin verb *dare* ('to give'), which in turn can be traced back to its Indo-European root **da*, also meaning 'to give'. The same root has given us words such as 'data' for information (literally 'things given'), 'donation', and even 'dice', the little cubes that are 'given' or thrown onto the gaming table. Another cognate word, frequently heard in former times but not so much now, was 'dowry', the money 'given' by a bride's father to her new husband.

Taking things a little bit further, the Latin *dare* also shows up in the Russian verb *dat'*. This also means 'to give' and is at the root of the word *dacha*, which anyone familiar with Russian literature will recognize as a cottage with a plot of land in the country where Russians like to relax at weekends and during the holidays. Such boltholes are so called because Peter the Great (r. 1682–1725) 'gave' out these plots in exchange for his subjects' loyal support.

b) 'Date' as the name of a fruit has travelled a long way through time and space to find its way into English. The word is derived from the ancient Greek *daktulos*, meaning 'finger' or 'toe', and the connection appears to be that in the ancient world people thought that the shape of the fruit (or perhaps its leaves) was not unlike that of a little finger or toe. The Indo-European root involved here is **dak* ('to hold'), and its association with fingers and toes needs no further explanation. Other words etymologically allied to the Greek *daktulos* include 'dactyl' (a metrical foot in poetry), and 'pterodactyl' (a flying dinosaur characterized by an elongated claw or finger at the end of each wing), and 'dactylography' (the scientific name for the study of fingerprints in the detection of criminals).

DIE

Examples: a) We all have to **die** eventually.
       b) The **die** is cast.

a) There is some discussion about just how old this verb is in English. There is evidence that it was used to a limited extent in Saxon times but is thought to have entered general use around the year 1200. Some linguists believe that this was due to the influence of foreign invaders, as Old Danish had *døja* and Old Norse had *deyja*, both of which were descended from the Proto-Germanic *dawjan* and the Indo-European *dheu* ('to become senseless').

In Old English the more common words were *steorfan* (this was related to the Indo-European root *ster* ('stiff') and originally meant 'to become stiff') and *sweltan*. The former is actually the modern 'starve', which since the 1570s has meant 'die of hunger' although in modern usage it frequently means merely 'to feel very hungry'. Its original meaning can still be seen in its modern German cognate *sterben* ('to die').

Sweltan is the origin of the modern verb 'swelter'. In Old English it signified death due to excessive heat but by the sixteenth century it had acquired its modern meaning 'to feel faint or just uncomfortable because of the heat'.

b) The expression 'the die is cast' meaning that an irreversible step has been taken is significant as it preserves the original singular form of the word. The cube used in games of chance is almost universally referred to as 'dice', 'the dice', and even 'a dice' as though the word were singular. But 'dice' is in fact the plural of 'die'.

By analogy with Spanish and Italian, which refer to the little cube as *dado* (literally 'given'), etymologists have concluded that the word is derived from the Latin *datum*, from the infinitive *dare*. This basically meant 'to give' but had secondary meanings of 'to play' and 'to move' in the gaming sense.

As a die was used in serious gambling sessions, it had to be absolutely straight and well balanced. A crooked die could lead to all sorts of misunderstandings and so needed to be perfectly regular in shape. This requirement is the origin of the associated phrase 'as straight as a die'. The original expression was 'as smooth as a die' (c. 1530); 'as straight as a die' and 'as true as a die' are later developments.

DIET

Examples: a) The doctor put him on a strict **diet** for two weeks.

b) The **Diet** of Worms was held in Germany.

a) The derivation of the word in this sense is open to a certain amount of discussion as its Greek and Latin origins seem to have combined and become somewhat confused over the centuries. It had been used in English to mean food in general since the thirteenth century and was applied to a specific regimen from the fourteenth century onwards. The Old French noun *diete* meaning 'fare', 'a diet', or a 'pittance' was acquired in the thirteenth century from the medieval Latin *dieta* meaning (i) a daily food allowance, (ii) a day's work, or (iii) a parliamentary assembly. All of these were developments of the Latin *diaeta* ('a prescribed way of life'), acquired from the Greek *diaita* ('a way of life'). No doubt this is the thinking behind the modern English use of the word; when we 'go on a diet' we have to adopt an entirely new lifestyle, at least as far as our food intake is concerned.

Some linguists, however, prefer the hypothesis that the origin of the word 'diet' goes back no further than the Latin *dies* meaning 'day'.

b) Thankfully, the word 'diet' as used in the term 'Diet of Worms' has absolutely nothing to do with eating wriggly invertebrates! In ancient Greek the reflexive verb *diaitasthai* meant 'to lead a certain way of life' but its non-reflexive form *diaitan* meant 'to support' or 'to maintain'. The verb had the secondary meaning of 'to act as an umpire' or 'to reconcile', and this led to the general meaning of 'to govern' and hence to the concept of an 'administrative assembly'.

The Diet of Worms was a deliberative assembly of the Holy Roman Empire based in Worms, a town to the south-west of Frankfurt. In 1521 Martin Luther was invited to appear before the assembly to defend his unorthodox views.

The *Oxford English Dictionary* gives the following additional meanings for the word 'diet': (i) a day's journey; (ii) an appointed day or time; and (iii) in the Royal Mint, since the seventeenth century, metal scraped off gold and silver on a daily basis during the assaying process.

DIKE

Examples: a) There was a **dike** in front of the castle.
           b) There are many **dikes** in Holland

a) This is an odd word. In the thirteenth century it referred to a trench in the ground, but by the fifteenth it denoted the embankment formed at the side of the ditch (an alternative word) with the excavated soil.

The Old English word for 'dike', *díc*, is cognate with the Dutch *dijk* ('dam'), and both are probably related to the modern English verb 'to dig'. The original English word here was *deolfan*, or, in its later form, 'to delve', but by the fourteenth century *deolfan* had been replaced by 'to dig' and survives today only figuratively in set expressions such as 'the police delved into the suspect's past in their search for evidence'.

b) 'Dike' as a term for a wall constructed to hold back water has a different history with some fascinating linguistic associations. It is descended from the Indo-European root **dheigh* ('to knead', 'to form', or 'to mould'). And one of the most primitive shapes to be moulded would have been some sort of earthwork or wall, as reflected in the cognate ancient Greek noun *teichos* ('wall'). Later on, other cognates appeared in various languages, all of them associated with the idea of moulding or shaping. Gothic had *digan* ('to mould', directly related to German *Teig* and Russian *testo*, both of which mean the same as, and are cognate with, the English noun 'dough').

In Anglo-Saxon times the word *hlæfdige* appeared, a combination of *hlæf* ('loaf') and *dæge* ('kneader'), which evolved into 'lady'. By comparison, the man who guarded the loaves once they had been made was in the *hlæfward*, which evolved into the word we now recognize as 'lord'. Just to complete the picture, the room where the 'loaf kneader' originally did her work was the 'dairy', a combination of *dæge* and the Old French suffix -*erie*, meaning 'the room where the dough is made'. The milkmaids were later arrivals.

DOWN

Examples: a) The South **Downs** are a beautiful part of England.

b) He came **down** the ladder too fast and fell on the floor.

c) Duck **down** pillows are very comfortable.

a) The term 'downs' has been applied to the low rolling countryside in parts of southern England since about 1300. As a geographical feature, they are basically undulating hills, and this is a clue to the origin of the term. It is closely associated with the prefixes -*tun*, -*dun*, -*ton*, etc, from the Proto-Germanic root **dunaz*, which itself seems to have originated in Celtic; Old Irish had *dun* for 'hill' or 'hill fort', and modern Welsh still has *dinas* for 'city'. The modern Welsh is of particular interest as it mirrors the development of the word in English. In Old English, a *dūn* was a 'hill', and a *tūn* was an 'enclosure', 'yard', 'farm', or 'estate', which by about the twelfth century had taken on the meaning of any group of buildings individually occupied by citizens and their families, or, in other words, a 'town'. The idea of an enclosure is also preserved in the modern German cognate noun *Zaun* ('fence').

In Old English the term for a large group of dwellings in an enclosed space was *burg* (from an Indo-European root**bhergh* meaning 'fortified place') which survives today in the word 'borough', used either as a separate noun or as a toponymic suffix.

b) The preposition and adverb 'down' is directly linked to the Old English word for a hill, *dūn*. The dative case of the noun was *dūne* and this was used either separately or in the phrase *af dūne*, literally meaning 'off the hill'. As motion 'off the hill' almost invariably indicates a direction from a higher position to a lower, the expression was eventually applied to any situation or movement involving descent.

c) The fluffy, soft plumage we refer to as 'down' is allied etymologically to the word 'dust'. The Indo-European root whence it came is **dhu* ('to shake' or 'to agitate'), which is also seen in the Old Norse *dunn* ('down') and its associate verb *dyja* ('to shake').

The eiderdown, a traditional bed covering in Britain, takes its name from the stuffing it contained, and this in turn was derived from the Icelandic for a large wild duck commonly found in northern European coastal regions, the *aeðr* ('eider'), plus the word *dunn*.

EGG

Examples: a) They had a boiled **egg** for breakfast every morning.
b) She **egged** him on to steal the money.

a) The spelling of the word 'egg' has changed considerably over the centuries, which must have caused a certain amount of confusion and misunderstanding in the Middle Ages. Until the sixteenth century it was spelled *eye* (plural *eyren*), although a northern dialect form, *egge*, had existed since the fourteenth century.

In Old English the word was *æg*, a descendant of Proto-Germanic **ajja* or **ajjaz*, related to the Indo-European root **owjom* ('egg'). This is probably also the derivation of the Greek *ōon* and Latin *ovum* (cognate with the word 'ovary') and may be ultimately connected to the Sanskrit *vís* and the Latin word *avis*, both of which mean 'bird'.

'Eye', referring to the organ of sight, is totally unconnected with the earlier spelling of 'egg'. It is ultimately descended from the Latin *oculus* and the Greek *okkos*, both of which meant 'eye'.

b) 'To egg on' as a verb meaning 'to urge' or 'to incite' is a very close relative, linguistically speaking, of the noun 'edge'. Clear evidence of this can be seen in the Old English spelling and pronunciation: the word would have been written *ecg* in Saxon times and pronounced 'edge'.

Old English *ecg* meant both 'a point' and 'a sword', which provides a clue to the derivation of the modern expression. Originally, 'to egg on' was 'to prod somebody' with a pointed stick or the tip of a sword until they agreed to whatever was being demanded of them.

Old Norse had the word *eggja* ('to goad' or 'to incite'), which was a derivative of the Indo-European **ak* ('to be sharp'), a root that shows up in many European languages and in some surprising places. It accounts for the German *Ecke* ('corner') and several words which have arrived in English via Greek, including 'acid', 'acrid', and 'acute'. It is even related to the 'Acropolis' in Athens, a collection of monuments whose name translates as 'city on a peak'.

FAIR

Examples: a) The weather was **fair** when we set sail for France.

b) All umpires and referees are supposed to be completely **fair**.

c) Dad took the kids to the **fair**.

a) It was not until the mid-sixteenth century that 'fair' was used to describe a pretty young lady's light complexion. Prior to that, it had been used from about 1200 to describe pleasant, as opposed to unpleasant, weather. Much earlier, Old English had *fæger* ('beautiful' or 'sweet') which developed into *feire* in Middle English, also meaning beautiful. But the roots from which these words evolved were the Germanic **fag* and the Indo-European **pak* ('to join' or 'to combine'). The original meaning of 'fair', therefore, was 'well constructed' (i.e., well put together), an idea reflected in another cognate adjective, the Greek *pēgos* ('firm', 'strong', 'compact', or 'well constructed').

b) The association of fairness with an unbiased attitude is not unrelated to the example above. Such an interpretation attached to the word 'fair' from the mid-fourteenth century and stemmed from the conviction that umpires had to be firm and resolute in their impartiality.

In about 1600 the expression 'fair and square' was coined to described people, decisions, and actions seen to be totally honest and without bias. The origin of this expression is not entirely certain; it might have been a carpenter's term for furniture which was firm and perfectly constructed or it could be an echo of the time (i.e., the sixteenth century) when 'square' was used as a synonym for 'honest'.

c) 'Fair' as a place of fun and amusement has its counterpart in the French *foire* and *fête*, both of which can be traced back to the Latin *feriae* ('festival' or 'holiday'). This in turn is derived from the noun *festum* ('celebration') and the adjective *festus* ('festive' or 'joyful').

Other cognate nouns include 'feast' (although the connotation of a sumptuous meal was a later development) and 'festoon'. We now use this as a synonym for 'drape', as when we talk of 'draping' or 'festooning' a room with garlands. No doubt the association here is with halls lavishly decorated with flowers at holidays (originally 'holy days'), festivals, and feasts.

FAN

Examples: a) She sat by the **fan** in order to keep cool.
           b) He is a great **fan** of Manchester United.

a) Whether handheld or powered by electricity, a 'fan' is the term for an artefact or instrument whose purpose is to generate a flow of air. The root of the word is the Indo-European **ua/*wan* ('to blow'), which occurs in English and other languages in words connected with currents of air. It is the root, for instance, behind English words such as 'wind' and 'weather', and both of these are related to the Sanskrit *vata* ('wind'). Cognate words in other European languages include the French, Spanish, and Italian for wind: *vent*, *viento*, and *vento* respectively. We also find it in a more distant linguistic cousin, the Russian word *veter*, which also means 'wind'.

The word 'fan' in its present form actually came into English in the fourteenth century, but previously it had occurred in Old English as *fann*, derived from the Latin *vannus*. In both Old English and Latin, the original meaning of the word was 'an instrument for winnowing grain (i.e., separating the wheat from the chaff). And the Latin verb for this process was *ventilare*, which, of course, has also given us the verb 'to ventilate'.

b) When we describe the staunch supporters of football clubs, pop stars, or idols of screen and stage as 'fans' we are using a word of a totally different derivation. 'Fan', in such cases, is a shortened form of the word 'fanatic', the origin of which is the Latin *fanum* meaning 'temple'. The adjective derived from it, *fanaticus*, was originally used to describe people inspired by a divinity and, in extreme cases, fixated on a religious idea to the exclusion of all reason. In the sixteenth century it was even applied to those thought to be insane. In milder cases, such people might have been described as being merely 'enthusiastic', a term for almost the same idea. It is derived from two Greek words *en* ('in') and *theos* ('god') and defines someone who 'has a god within him or her'.

The use of 'fan' to denote an 'avid supporter' originated in the United States in the nineteenth century.

FARE

Examples: a) '**Fare** thee well' used to be a common expression in English.

b) She paid the **fare** when she got on the bus.

a) There are several meaning of the word 'fare', and all are derived from the basic word meaning 'to go'. The Germanic root **fer* spawned Old English *faran*, Middle English *faren*, as well as the modern German *fahren*, all of which mean 'to travel'. The verb no longer exists with this meaning in English but it does survive in a surprising number of cognate nouns and set expressions. 'Fare thee well' is now considered archaic, but the shorter version 'farewell', if not very common, is still heard, particularly in songs or poetry. It was originally a term used on parting, when the sense was really 'may you enjoy a safe journey'. Another term for a traveller, 'wayfarer' is now hardly ever encountered and survives only in older forms of the language, but its nautical equivalent, 'seafarer', is still heard. Also in current use are expressions such as 'thoroughfare', a road; 'welfare', a synonym for well-being; and 'warfare', originally the practice of 'travelling about' waging war.

b) The concept of travel is preserved in other current uses of the word. To pay a 'fare' is to pay whatever is the requisite amount in order to be able to travel on a bus, train, etc. Over time, the word has come to refer not only to the money paid but to the person paying, although this usage now tends to be restricted to taxis, where a passenger is regularly referred to as 'a fare'.

Another extension of this use is associated with food. It is quite common to refer to victuals on offer at a particular establishment as 'fare'. 'Fine fare' or 'traditional fare' are not uncommon descriptions of good food provided by a restaurant or for sale in a supermarket. Originally, however, the 'fare' would probably have been food prepared in advance to sustain a traveller on a journey.

But the most surprising cognate is probably the word 'elver'. This is now used as a term to designate young eels and has been used in this form since the seventeenth century. In the sixteenth century the form 'eel-vare' appeared, a southern English pronunciation of 'eel-fare', the term for a brood of young eels. Originally, however, the term referred to the passage or journey of young eels as they made their way up a stream or river.

FAST

Examples: a) The door is **fast** and won't open.

b) He can run almost as **fast** as his big brother.

c) She decided to **fast** for a few days in order to lose weight.

a) The concept of 'fast' meaning 'immobile', seems to be diametrically opposed to the idea of speed. But the consensus of linguistic opinion is that they are related. The Old English *fæst*, Old Norse *fastr*, and Middle English *fast* all meant 'firm' or 'resolute' and survive in expressions such as 'steadfast' (literally 'standing firm'), 'to be fast asleep', and 'to hold fast'. It is also, of course, the root of the verbs 'to fasten' and 'to unfasten'.

b) Fast as a synonym of 'quick' needs a little explaining. If a person is follow-ing another who is walking or running rapidly the one behind has to make a determined effort to keep up. We might say, in other words, that he has to keep 'steadfastly' on his heels. At some point in the sixteenth century the word 'fast' came to be associated with the speed needed to keep up with the person in front rather than with the determination not to be left behind.

The implication of wantonness and dissipation (e.g., 'fast living', 'a fast woman') is a seventeenth century usage.

c) Originally associated with religious observance, the practice of 'fasting' is related etymologically to the above examples. The reasoning here is that the person concerned would adhere firmly (or 'hold fast') to the rules and regu-lations of a religious order governing how long and under what conditions a believer should refrain from eating. By the twelfth century 'fast' could be used both as a verb (to fast) and as a noun (a fast). When those who laid down the rules decided that the period of fasting was at an end, it was a signal for the peni-tents to 'break their fast'. And this has given us the modern English 'breakfast'.

FENCE

Examples: a) She grew a Virginia creeper along the **fence**.

b) Frank learned to **fence** while still at school.

c) The thief needed to find a **fence** for the stolen jewels.

a) A 'fence', usually a wooden structure dividing one garden or plot of land from another, was originally for protection as can be seen from its associated infinitive 'to defend'. It is originally from the Latin *defendere* ('to ward off'), which is itself comprised of *de* ('off' or 'away') and an assumed root **fendo* ('I strike'). It was obviously taken for granted in the ancient world that almost any form of defence would involve the use of force of one sort or another.

The Latin word for a defensive wall was *moenia*, and its associated verb, *munire*, meant 'to build a wall' or 'to surround with a wall'. By the sixteenth century the derivative noun *munition* had appeared in Middle French referring not only to a protective wall but also to the additional paraphernalia required for engaging in defensive battle. However, *la munition* was misheard by the common soldiery and rendered *l'ammunition*, adopted and adapted by the English as 'ammunition'. The result is that in English we can now speak of both 'ammunition' and 'munitions'.

b) Personal protection by means of a sword has only been referred to as 'fencing' since the 1580s. In the modern world its use is limited to a sporting context as modern warfare has made prowess with the blade on the battlefield more than just a little redundant.

A 'sword', the basic weapon of defence in former times, was *sweard* or *swyrd* in Old English and is cognate with the modern German *Schwert*. They are all thought to be derived from Old High German **swertha* ('a cutting weapon'). Interestingly, the weapon known as the 'sabre' has a similar derivation. It entered most European languages from the Hungarian *szablya*, a noun related to the verb *szabni* ('to cut').

c) The shady character in the world of crime known as a 'fence' has been around for a long time. The word was part of thieves' slang in 1700 and referred to the men (and possibly women) who operated under the 'defence of anonymity' as they surreptitiously, but no doubt profitably, disposed of stolen goods.

FIDDLE

Examples: a) Many a good tune is played on an old **fiddle**, or so they say.

b) The boy had a tendency to **fiddle** about in class.

c) The clerk tried to **fiddle** the books and was arrested.

a) There is a certain amount of snobbery attached to this word. Classical musicians would always refer to their instrument as a 'violin', but a folk group could set people's feet tapping with a jaunty tune played on a fiddle or two. Strangely, however, they are both variants of the same word.

The Germanic languages all have a form of the word close to the English spelling. Old English had *fiðele*, Old Norse had *fiðla*, Old High German had *fidula*, and modern German has *Fiedel*. In the fourteenth century Middle English had several versions: *fedele*, *fydyll*, and *fidel*.

The Latin word from which the word has evolved was *vitula* ('calf'). But Vitula was also the Roman goddess of victory, mirth, and rejoicing who produced the associated verb *vitulari* ('to celebrate'). Obviously no celebration would have been complete without music and dancing, and the instrument chosen to add a musical dimension was termed the *vitula*, presumably because of its association with victory celebrations and the calf that provided the feast.

Vitula evolved in the Romance languages as *viole* in French and *viola* in Italian and Spanish with their diminutives *violon*, *violino*, and *violín* respectively. In other words, 'fiddle' and 'violin' are simply Germanic and Romance versions of the same word.

b) Playing the fiddle must have appeared to some people in the sixteenth century as a bit of a waste of time. By the middle of the sixteenth century the word 'fiddle-faddle' had appeared to denote trifles or matters of minimal importance. A century later this had become a verb meaning 'to concern oneself with trifles', and pretty soon afterwards it was being used to describe pointless activity.

c) The totally unconnected association of the word with dishonest or even criminal activity is believed to stem from an American English verb of the 1920s 'finagle'. This in turn is thought to be from the English dialect word 'fainaigue' (to cheat at cards). Ultimately, however, this is probably from 'feign' and 'ague', which together meant 'to pretend to be ill' in order to be excused from work.

FILE

Examples: a) She found her scissors and comb but not her nail **file**.
b) His secretary found the **file** containing the documents.
c) The boys were marching along the road in single **file**.

a) The first meaning of the noun 'file', an instrument for paring down nails, metal, or wood, is from the Indo-European root **pik* or **peik* (basically meaning 'to cut' or 'to carve'). Over time the meaning evolved somewhat and came to include the less dramatic practice of gradually wearing down. But there is another rather surprising connection here. The same root was associated with processes of adornment, either by cutting, painting, or carving, and shows up in words such as 'picture', 'pigment', and even the beautiful, brightly coloured little bird, the 'finch'. And if we look a little further afield we find the same root in the Russian verb *pisat'*, which originally meant 'to paint' but now has acquired the additional meaning of 'to write'.

b) The file associated with the item of office furniture, the 'filing cabinet', is of a very different history. Its root is the Latin *filum*, which simply means 'thread'. The connection here is not immediately obvious until we remember that in Roman times the simplest way of a making sure documents did not get lost would have been to tie them together with whatever was used as string in those days. Over the centuries, as more and more documents were produced and threading them together became impractical, they would have been stored in a box or cabinet of some description. Thus the basic idea behind what we now refer to as a 'filing cabinet' was born.

c) As far as we know, the first reference to soldiers in a column described as 'marching in file' appeared at the end of the sixteenth century. Presumably the association is with a line of soldiers resembling a length of thread.

FIRE

Examples: a) **Fire** engulfed the whole house, but everyone was saved.
            b) Her boss had to **fire** her when she was caught stealing.

a) The word 'fire' exists in varying forms in most European languages: French has *feu*, German has *Feuer*, Spanish has *fuego*, and Italian, *fuoco*. They all trace their origins back to the Indo-European **pu* or **pur*, a root associated with brightness and cleanliness. In fact, a brief glance at the Greek and Latin words descended from the same root illustrates the strong connection noted in ancient times between fire and its power to purify. The very word 'purify' (along with 'purge' and 'pure') is a derivative of the Latin *purus* ('pure'), which itself is cognate with the Greek *pur* ('fire'), usually transliterated as 'pyro-' in prefixes. The same link can be seen in the Roman Catholic Church's concept of 'purgatory' (from the Latin *purgare* ('to cleanse')), which since the thirteenth century has been postulated by the Church as the place where souls are 'purged' of their sins before they ascend to heaven.

It is interesting to note the interplay between the initial letters 'p' and 'f' in the various European languages. English has retained both variants, depending on the circumstances: the everyday word is 'fire', but it is usual to talk about a funeral 'pyre'; we set off celebratory 'fireworks', but the science of how they behave is 'pyrotechnics'; and the psychological condition resulting in an excessive fascination with fire is 'pyromania'.

b) The use of the word to describe what happens when an employee is dismissed from his or her job dates back to the 1880s and was first used in American English. The original concept, however, can be traced back several centuries to the time when guns and cannons were being used with increasing regularity on the field of battle. The expression 'to fire' a weapon was in use in the first half of the sixteenth century and soon became synonymous with the idea of 'discharging', which since the fourteenth century had generally meant 'to disburden' or 'to relieve' but had now also acquired specific military connotations. At some time in the nineteenth century, an imaginative American apparently noticed the similarity between 'relieving' a firearm of its charge and 'relieving' a member of the workforce of his or her duties.

FLEET

Examples: a) James sailed with the **fleet** just before dawn.
           b) She was **fleet** of foot and won all the races.

a) The Indo-European **pleu* is arguably one of the most prolific roots. It lies behind many words in English (as well as several other European languages) and is usually connected with water in some way. It accounts for the Russian *plyt'* ('to swim' or 'to sail'), the French *pleuvoir* ('to rain'), as well as the Greek verbs *plein* ('to sail' or 'to swim') and *plunein* ('to wash'). In the Germanic languages the consonants 'pl' changed to 'fl' and produced a whole host of nouns and verbs: 'to flow', 'a fleet', 'to float', and, although the medium is air instead of water, 'to fly' and the insect 'a fly'.

This root's association with things watery also gave the Anglo-Saxons their word for 'to float', 'to drift', or 'to swim', *fleotan*, in addition to the word for 'boat', *fleot*, which was eventually expanded to designate a group of ships, a 'fleet'. This was the normal term for an assembly of warships prior to 1200 when, under the influence of Norman French, the word 'navy' (originally from the Latin *navis* ('ship')) found its way into English. The result is that in modern English the words 'fleet' and 'navy' are synonymous. Interestingly, however, we speak of the Royal Navy but its highest ranking officer is the Admiral of the Fleet.

A now archaic use of the word in English was as a synonym for the words 'stream', 'brook', etc, surviving in a few English place names such as the famous Fleet Street in London. This has nothing to do with the Royal Navy but serves as a reminder that very close to what is now a concrete jungle there used to be a stream known locally as 'the fleet'.

b) The association with speed is of particular interest. To the ancients, fast-flowing rivers, streams, etc., symbolized rapidity of movement to such an extent that they associated them with speed in general. In Old Norse, the word *fliotr* meant 'fast' and came from the same Indo-European root as 'flow'. This link has survived into modern English and can be seen in expressions such as 'a fleeting moment' and 'a fleeting memory' where the brevity of duration is likened to the movement of a fast-flowing stream.

FLOCK

Examples: a) A **flock** pillow can be very comfortable to sleep on.
　　　　　 b) The shepherd watches over his **flock**.

a) The Old French *floc* and Middle English *flocke* were both derivatives of the Latin *floccus* meaning a wisp of wool or hair. And all three words are cognate with the ancient Greek *phladō* (or *phlaō*) 'I tear', suggesting that the original meaning of 'flock' was a tuft or handful of wool 'torn off' a larger pile.

The word is also perhaps related to the more modern word 'frock', although this too has changed in meaning over the centuries. Originally (i.e., in the twelfth century) a frock was only a monk's habit and was not used of women's outer garments until the early or middle part of the sixteenth century.

The Latin *floccus* was also used by the Romans to suggest insignificance or worthlessness.

b) The original Old English word for a large group of cattle or sheep was *heord* (modern English 'herd'), a descendant of the Indo-European **kerdh* ('group'). At some point *flocc* made its appearance in Old English, a direct borrowing from the Old Norse *flokkr* ('troop' or 'band'). Its application to domestic animals such as sheep dates from around 1300. A few years later (c. 1350) the word acquired a more spiritual meaning and was used metaphorically to designate the followers of Christ. An interesting parallel can be seen here in the use of the word 'congregation' to describe those who attend Christian church services. The root of this word is *grex*, the Latin for 'flock'.

It has not been conclusively proven, but there is also a theory that the word 'folk' is a variant of 'flock'.

FONT

Examples: a) The old church had a particularly fine **font**.

              b) He never changed the default **font** on his computer.

a) Most Christian churches throughout the world feature a 'font' or receptacle (usually made of stone) containing the water used during baptism (from the Greek *baptein* ('to dip')). In medieval Latin, the term for this architectural device was *fons baptismalis* ('baptismal font'), the origin of the word as it now appears in English, 'font'.

In medieval Latin, the closely related term *fontana* was applied to any refreshing stream of water that flowed out naturally from beneath the earth. This produced variations in several European languages: French has *fontaine*, Russian *fontan*, German *Fontane*, and English 'fountain'. Spanish curiously has *surtidor* for 'fountain' but retains the word *fontanero* for 'plumber', the man whose job it is to install and maintain the water supply in buildings and homes.

There is a surprising cognate noun in the world of anatomy: the gap in the skull of a newly born child is referred to medically as the 'fontanelle', a reference to the opening in the bone structure which reminded the early (c. eighteenth century) medical practitioners of the hole in the ground from which a 'fountain' flowed.

b) Since the arrival of personal computers and word processors the word 'font', formerly the preserve of printers, has become far more widely used among the general public. The word's association with letter formations and designs dates from the early days of printing when individual letters had to be formed from molten metal poured into a mould. English acquired the word (via Old French) from the Latin *fundere* ('to pour' or 'to pour out'), the infinitive which also produced the word 'fount', formerly an alternative to the word 'font'. The connection here with processing molten metal can be seen in the modern English 'foundry'. Since the seventeenth century this has been the term for a workshop where molten metal is transformed into useful or decorative artefacts.

GIN

Examples: a) John had a beer, and his wife had a **gin** and tonic.

b) The poacher got his foot caught in a **gin**.

a) According to popular etymology, the spirit we know as 'gin' takes its name from the Swiss city Geneva. But this is pure myth. The word came into English from Old French *genevre*, which coincidentally and confusingly resembled the French for Geneva, Genève. But in fact it is a corruption of the Latin word *iuniperus* ('juniper tree'). And just for the record, the Swiss city was named Genava by the Romans who adapted the Celtic *genawa* ('estuary' or 'bend in a river'). This evolved eventually into the modern spelling.

b) In the thirteenth century 'gins' were used for snaring animals, and landowners soon realized that they could also be used for deterring trespassers and keeping unbidden guests off their land. Such mantraps have thankfully long been declared illegal in Britain and consigned to the darker reaches of our social history.

The word 'gin' is actually a contraction of 'engine', a borrowing and corruption of the Latin *ingenium* which really was a reference to a person's natural or inborn abilities. By a process of association, it came to signify any product of this innate talent, rather than the talent itself.

It is also related to the word 'genius', originally the definition of a man or woman blessed with a gift for inventing things. Nowadays, however, a 'genius' can be anyone who demonstrates an unusual degree of skill in almost any field of human activity.

The 'gen' element of *ingenium*, of course, is related to words associated with birth such as 'genesis', 'genus', and 'generate', all of which are derived ultimately from the Greek verb *gignesthai* ('to become' or 'to be born').

GORGE

Examples: a) 'Don't **gorge** your food,' said his mother.

b) Last year on holiday we drove past the Cheddar **Gorge**.

a) The use of the word as a verb meaning 'to eat greedily' has featured in English since the fourteenth century. As a noun it has acquired several similar meanings with the passage of time: in the fifteenth century it meant the craw of a hawk; by the sixteenth century it was applied to the contents of the stomach; and by the eighteenth it was synonymous with 'ravine'.

The word entered English from Old French, which had *gorge* ('throat' or 'bosom'), borrowed from late Latin *gurges* ('gullet'), a word which in classical Latin had meant 'whirlpool' or 'abyss', possibly connected to *gurgulio* ('gullet' or 'windpipe'). The root of each seems to be the Indo-European **gwere* ('to swallow').

There is some discussion among etymologists as to whether or not the adjective 'gorgeous' is linguistically linked to the noun 'gorge'. Proponents of the theory base their argument on the ancient habit of wearing a gorget. This was originally a piece of armour designed to protect the neck and throat, but over time it became less a defensive device and more a fashion item. The more intricate, flamboyant, and expensive looking the gorgets became, the more attractive they were said to be. And those who wore beautiful neckwear soon came to be known as 'gorgeous' themselves.

b) The place in Somerset, England known as the Cheddar Gorge is completely tautological. The village of Cheddar was originally (AD 880) known as Ceodre, a name derived from the Old English word *ceodor* ('gorge' or 'ravine').

GRATE

Examples: a) The strident music soon began to **grate** on me.
                   b) The coals were heaped up in the **grate**.

a) The figurative use of the verb 'to grate' reflects the literal meaning of 'scraping' or 'scratching', associated with the Middle English verb *graten*. It is also related to the Old French *grater* and modern French *gratter* ('to scrape' or 'to scratch'). Anything unpleasant described as 'grating' on us is a figurative reminder of the unpleasant sensation experienced when our skin is being scraped. The derivative medieval Latin verb here was *gratare* or its variant *cratare* ('to scrape'), unsurprisingly connected linguistically with the modern French description *au gratin* for any dish topped with 'grated' cheese or bread crumbs. Ultimately the word is thought to be Germanic in origin.

b) 'Grate' as a noun was the term used in the fourteenth century for the iron grills used when meat was being cooked over a fire. By the fifteenth century it was also applied to the ironwork placed in front of doors and windows to provide greater security and protection for the inhabitants. The Middle English word *grate* was derived from the vulgar Latin *grata*, which had an earlier form *crata* (hence the cognate noun 'crate'), from the Latin *cratis* ('wicker basket', 'frame', or 'harrow'). It is also the origin of the English word 'hurdle', a derivation which warrants particular explanation.

The Sanskrit *krt* ('to bind' or 'to spin') produced the Greek *kurtia* ('wicker-work') and the Latin *cratis*, which evolved into the Old High German *hurt* and the Old English *hyrd* ('door') and its diminutive form of *hyrdel*. This then evolved into the modern English 'hurdle', the original meaning of which was simply a framework of twigs that had been 'bound' together.

The Old English *hyrd* is also connected with the modern English term 'hoarding', the temporary fencing frequently erected around a vacant plot of land.

GRAVE

Examples: a) The coffin was slowly lowered into the **grave**.

b) The officer made a **grave** error.

a) We now use the word 'grave' to describe the elongated hole dug in the ground in which a coffin is buried. In Anglo-Saxon times the word was *græf*, cognate with German *graben* and Dutch *graven* (both meaning 'to dig'). All three of these words are related to other English words such as 'groove' and the verb 'to engrave', which implies nothing more than making a series of grooves in a piece of stone or metal. If we follow the lead back a bit further in time we find that 'grave' is also related to the ancient Greek word *graphein* ('to write') and the association becomes clearer still when we consider that an even earlier meaning of *graphein* was 'to scratch'. As the first attempts at writing involved nothing more than 'scratching' or 'engraving' letters on a clay tablet or in wet sand with a pointed implement, it is easy to understand the connection.

b) Totally unconnected with 'digging' or 'scratching' is the adjective 'grave', which is simply a synonym for 'serious' or 'important'. This word has come down to us from the Latin *gravis*, the primary meaning of which was 'heavy' but it later acquired additional meanings of solemnity and seriousness. A related noun which is sometimes seen in English is 'gravitas'.

The Indo-European root from which the Latin adjective was derived is **gru/*gwer* which is also the origin of the Sanskrit *gurus* ('important'). This is turn gave us the word *guru*, which we now understand as referring either to a Hindu religious leader or someone who can speak with authority on a given subject.

The same origins are also responsible for words and expressions such as 'gravity', the force which makes objects feel heavy; 'elderly primigravida', a medical term applied to women who have their first pregnancy later than usual; and the verb 'to aggravate', the original meaning of which was simply 'to make heavier'.

GROSS

Examples: a) She ordered a **gross** of eggs from the farmer.

b) The officer stood accused of **gross** misconduct.

c) He was offered a very attractive **gross** salary.

a) All the meanings associated with this word date back to about the fourth century AD. The adjective *grossus* did not exist in classical Latin but suddenly appeared in late Latin as an adjective describing anything excessively large, thick, or stout. All attempts to trace the word's origins further back in time have proven fruitless and the most that can be said is that *grossus* might have been borrowed from a Celtic source.

Its specific use as a noun to denote twelve dozen of anything dates from the fifteenth century and entered English from Old French which had the expression *grosse dozeine* ('fat dozen'), commonly in use among traders and merchants. As such traders normally dealt in bulk purchases and sales, they came to be known as *grossiers* (from the medieval Latin for 'wholesaler', *grossarius*), the origin of the modern English term 'grocer'. In modern English, the term applies to food retailers and is a particularly common designation for those who trade in fruit and vegetables, usually referred to as 'greengrocers'.

The idea of large quantities has given rise to a rather surprising related expression: 'to be engrossed in'. If we say that we are 'engrossed' in a certain activity, we are letting people know that whatever it is we are doing is taking up the 'bulk' of our time and energies.

b) Despite the fact that 'gross' is cognate with the ordinary French *gros* ('large'), its use in modern English has acquired overtones of coarseness, excess and always suggests unattractiveness. It is seldom used now to describe people, but has more figurative uses such as 'gross error', 'gross misjudgement', etc. More generally, if we describe something as 'gross' we are making a strong suggestion that we find it disgusting and totally undesirable.

c) Wages and salaries are frequently quoted as being either 'gross' or 'net'. In this context the use of the word 'gross' indicates that the sum quoted is the 'large' figure quoted before the normal deductions such as taxes and pension contributions have been taken into consideration.

GUM

Examples: a) He has a **gum** infection and is taking antibiotics.

b) Miss Jones does not like people chewing **gum** in class.

a) In modern English, the word 'gum' has a precise anatomical meaning; it refers solely to the firm fleshy tissue through which the teeth grow. In former times, however, things were not quite so simple. The Old English *gōma* could refer to the palate, the side of the mouth or the lining of the throat. In the plural, *gōman*, it meant 'jaws'.

'Gum' is distantly related to and cognate with the Greek verb *khainein* ('to yawn', 'to open the mouth', or 'to gape (of wounds)') as well as to *khasma*, also seen in modern English but now spelled 'chasm'. A further cognate Greek noun is *khaos*, spelled in modern English as 'chaos', now used to denote a scene of total disorder. But to the poet Hesiod (c. 700 BC), *khaos* was the 'yawning' chasm of infinite space that existed before the cosmos came into being.

The literal meaning of 'cosmos' (*kosmos* to the Greeks) was 'order' and its derivative adjective *kosmētos* meant 'ordered' or 'well arranged'. Its associated noun in modern English is 'cosmetics', literally nothing more than powders and creams designed to restore order.

b) The sticky substance exuded by some trees and plants and also known as 'gum' has taken a long and tortuous route into modern English. Old French had *gome*, derived from the Latin *gummi*, but this in turn was derived from the Greek *kommi*. And *kommi* was almost certainly acquired from Egyptian Arabic *kemai*, related to *komē* in Coptic, the official language of Egypt until around the thirteenth century.

'Chewing gum', the resinous sticky substance sold as a popular item of confectionary, was first attested in the United States in 1842.

HAIL

Examples: a) The wind and **hail** drove them all indoors.

b) John would often **hail** me from the other side of the street.

a) The frozen rain which can suddenly 'hail down' from the heavens was known in Old English by a variety of spellings: *hagel, haegel,* and *haegl.* They can all be traced back to Latin and ancient Greek words denoting or associated with little stones. In Latin *calx* meant 'a stone' and another related noun, *calculus,* was the word for a 'pebble' or 'small stone'. A little further back, Greek had two words for 'pebble', *khalix* and *kakhlēx.* Interestingly, both the Greek words, when used in a collective sense, meant 'rubble', 'gravel', or even 'rubbish' (i.e., for filling in gaps when building a wall or similar structure). The Latin term for this was *caementum,* the origin of the English 'cement'.

'Little stones' (or *calculi*) were used by the Romans for counting and the practice gave us the verb 'to calculate' as well as the noun 'calculus'. And the same word can also be seen in the medical term 'calculus', known colloquially as a kidney stone.

b) 'Hail' meaning 'to greet' and its homophone 'hale' (healthy) are very close linguistic relatives.

As a synonym for 'greeting' it dates from around the year AD 1200 and is Scandinavian in origin. Old Norse had *heill* for 'good luck' 'health' and 'prosperity'. A direct descendent can be seen in the Old English *waes haeil* literally meaning 'be healthy' and surviving even into modern English as the Christmas custom of 'wassailing'. This normally involves raising a glass of mulled wine and wishing one's fellow men health and good fortune for the coming year. It also has a less fortunate historical echo, however, in that it is the same word that showed up in the Nazi salute *Heil Hitler!* ('Hail (i.e., health to) Hitler!').

The description of somebody of a jolly disposition as 'hail-fellow-well-met' is thought to have entered English in the late sixteenth century.

HELM

Examples: a) The knight took off his **helm** after the joust.

b) She grabbed the **helm** and steered the boat over the rapids.

a) The word 'helm' is now only found in poetry, and its more usual form 'helmet' is really a fifteenth century French word *helmet,* the diminutive of the

Old French *helme* (for which the modern French is *heaume*). In other words, our 'helmet' is really just a 'little helm'. The Indo-European root at play here is **kel*, which is responsible for a host of words associated with covering, hiding, and concealment, and a 'helmet', of course, is nothing more than something that covers the head. The same root produced the Latin *celare* ('to conceal') and its derivative *cella*, a small room or storeroom where objects could be kept hidden away from prying eyes. Other cognate words used in modern English include 'cell', 'cellar', 'ceiling', and even 'hell'. Religion has given us a vision of hell as a place of everlasting torture, but linguistically speaking it is nothing more than a place 'hidden' away from us.

In Greek, the Indo-European root **kel* produced the verb *kaluptein* ('to cover') seen in two words known to modern English: (i) the 'eucalyptus' tree, so called because its buds are unusually 'well covered'; and (ii) the biblical book of the 'Apocalypse' (or Revelation), so called because it is supposed to deal with the 'uncovering' of God's intentions.

b) Since the thirteenth century 'helm' has been used in English as an alternative to 'tiller', although it existed in Old English as *helma* ('rudder'). Its Proto-Germanic antecedent was **halbma*, from the Indo-European root **kelp* ('to grasp' or 'to hold'). A modern if rather uncommon cognate noun is 'helve' (the handle of an axe or weapon). Yet another cognate, and one which is far more commonly encountered in English, is 'halter'. As a piece of equipment for keeping control of horses, the word existed in Old English as *hælftre* and meant nothing more than 'something to hold on to'.

HIDE

Examples: a) I decided to **hide** my money under the bed.
b) The buffalo is known to have a very tough **hide**.
c) The Domesday Book often mentions **hides**.

a) Old English had the verb *hydan* ('to hide', 'to cover', or 'to conceal'), a verb with its origins in the Indo-European root **keudh*, which also produced the Greek *keuthein* ('to hide' or 'to conceal'). Interestingly, the Old English *hydan* also meant 'to bury a corpse' and the Greek *keuthein* had the additional specific meaning of 'to wrap in a shroud'. The concept of a final 'hiding' place would appear to be the common denominator.

b) Directly associated with the idea of concealment is the word 'hide' when applied to animal skins. The Old English verb *hydan* ('to conceal') was closely related to *hyd* ('covering skin'), a noun cognate with the modern German *Haut* (also 'skin').

There are several cognates linked with this Old English noun. The Indo-European root **keudh* also produced the Greek *kutos* ('skin' or 'cover') and *skutos* ('leather'). Derivative nouns here are the Latin *cutis* ('skin'), *scutum* ('shield'), and the noun *scutarius* ('shield bearer'), which evolved into the modern English 'esquire' and 'squire'. It is also possibly the source of the Old English *hūs*, which is the origin of the most important 'covering' for anyone: a 'hut' or 'house'.

c) The 'hide' as a measured area of land is now more of historical than modern social interest, but it still holds a certain fascination for the linguist. In Anglo-Saxon society a *higid* or *hīd* (related to the Old English *hīwen* ('family' or 'household')) was either the basic unit of land considered necessary to support a man and his family or the area of land that could be tilled in one year by one man and his plough. In all probability the truth is a combination of the two ideas.

The word *hīd* was derived from the Indo-European root **kei* ('to lie'), as was the adjective 'quiet'. A possible interpretation here is that where a man's *hīd* 'lay' was where he sought peace and 'quiet' away from the clamour of everyday life.

HOST

Examples: a) Wordsworth spoke of a '**host** of golden daffodils'.

b) Peter was reputed to be a very jovial **host**.

c) The **Host** is the consecrated bread of the Eucharist.

a) As a synonym for 'multitude' this word has been used in English since the mid-thirteenth century. It was adopted from the Old French *host* ('army'), which in turn came from the medieval Latin *hostis* ('army' or 'military expedition'). By the early seventeenth century the word was being applied generally to mean simply any 'large number'.

In classical Latin *hostis* meant either 'an enemy' or simply 'a stranger'.

b) The use of the term to denote someone who receives guests dates from the late thirteenth century and came into English from Old French *hoste* (modern French *hôte*), which could variously mean 'guest', 'host', or 'landlord'. The linguistic ancestor of this word was the Latin *hospes* (genitive *hospitis*) meaning either 'friend', 'guest', or 'stranger'. Similarly, the Old English derivative *giest* could mean 'guest', 'enemy', or 'stranger'.

This of course is very confusing and it has spawned some surprising linguistic offspring. For instance, the words 'host' and 'guest', despite defining totally different social roles, share the same etymology. Also, the adjectives 'hospitable' (welcoming to strangers) and 'hostile' (aggressively opposed to strangers) are derived from the same Latin noun. But we do not have to look very far for an explanation of this apparent contradiction: in ancient times strangers would always be seen initially as at least potential enemies until they proved that their intentions were not 'hostile'. Then they could be welcomed as 'guests' and treated perhaps to lavish 'hospitality'.

Other common cognate words include 'hospice', 'hostel' and 'hotel'. Interestingly, the word 'hospital' was originally devoid of any medical associations and meant nothing more than 'a large house', from the Latin plural noun *hospitalia* ('apartments for strangers'). It only became a place of refuge for the sick in the sixteenth century.

c) The Host used in church services is of a totally unrelated derivation. It is from the Latin *hostia*, the term used for the victim in the days when sacrifice formed part of religious ceremonies. Related to an earlier form in Latin, the original term was *fostia* ('that which has been slain'), derived from the verb *fostire* ('to strike').

INCENSE

Examples: a) A smell of **incense** filled the whole church.

               b) She was **incensed** when she heard the news.

a) The Latin word *incendium* ('conflagration' or 'fire') was derived from the verb *incendere* ('to set on fire'). This had a secondary derivative noun, *incensum*, which could be applied to just about anything that had been burnt. It was adopted into French as *encens* and then, in the late thirteenth century, the word crossed the Channel and appeared in English in the form we know today.

A close relative here is the word 'frankincense', a combination of the Old French *franc* 'pure' and *encens* (i.e., incense of the highest quality). It is not recorded in English before the fourteenth century and yet most of us know of it only as one of the gifts taken to Christ as he lay in a manger in Bethlehem. The word used in the Greek version of the event is *libanos*, which is echoed in the resin's alternative name, Oil of Lebanon.

The practice of burning sweet-smelling herbs has long been associated with religion and the act of worship. In the 1880s the expression 'joss sticks' (i.e., Chinese incense) found its way into English; this was a corruption of the Javanese *dejos*, itself a borrowing from the sixteenth-century Portuguese *deos* or *deus* ('god') and ultimately cognate with the Greek *Zeus*.

There is, however, a further Greek connection with the practice of burning fragrant leaves for religious purposes. The verb *thuein* meant 'to worship', and the herb burned to help prayers rise to heaven was called *thumos*. This eventually made its way into Middle French as *thym* (pronounced 'teem') and then into English. This is the origin of the herb we now refer to as 'thyme'.

b) At some point early in the fifteenth century the verb 'to incense' acquired a figurative meaning synonymous with 'causing extreme anger'. The implication was that anger engendered heat and heat would make the person involved glow with fury. The original Latin verb *candescere* ('to glow white with heat'), related to *incendere*, also gave us the words 'candle' and, surprisingly, 'candidate'. The explanation for this is that in ancient Rome a citizen would normally wear a *candida toga* ('a gleaming white toga') if he was seeking office or election to an important civic post. Such a person would then be described as *candidatus* ('clothed in shining white'), and even though the custom of donning such a garment has been consigned to history, the derivative noun 'candidate' is still with us.

INVEST

Examples: a) It was decided to **invest** the bishop in January.

b) 'How much do you wish to **invest**?' asked the banker.

c) The troops were ordered to **invest** the town.

a) The original idea of 'to invest' was 'to clothe', and all other meanings have developed from this. In the late fourteenth century the verb 'invest' was used to define the act of bestowing the official robes of office on important personages, and although the verb is not in common use today, we do still refer to the ceremony as an 'investiture'. The Latin verb which is the origin of the term was *investire* from *in* ('on') and *vestire* ('to clothe', 'to surround', or 'to cover'), a survival of which is the modern 'vest'. This was originally a loose-fitting outer garment but since the nineteenth century has referred to an article of men's underwear.

'Vest' and the Latin *vestire* are cognate with the verb 'to wear', which appeared as *werian* in Old English and *verja* in Old Norse, both allied to the Proto-Germanic **wazjan* and the Indo-European **wes/*was* ('to put on'). Another cognate Latin noun was *vestis*, which could refer to any of the following: (i) a covering, (ii) a blanket, (iii) an awning, (iv) a carpet or tapestry, (v) the skin of a snake, or (vi) a spider's web.

b) The commercial organization known as the East India Company is thought to have been responsible for the first use of the verb 'to invest' in the world of finance. The basic idea here is that a person or a company might have a certain amount of cash which they wish to convert into a form of profit-making enterprise different from (or additional to) their usual areas of business activity. In other words, they want to disguise their wealth (i.e., 'cover it up'), and by 1740 this usually meant putting it into property speculation.

A further commercial, if archaic, use of the verb 'to vest' implied the settlement of land, goods, money, etc., in the possession of another person. Once a deal had been reached there was to be no further discussion, but the persons concerned were said to have a 'vested interest' in any profits likely to accrue from the agreement.

c) The military use of the verb 'to invest' meaning 'to besiege' is not very common today, but it was used with this meaning in English at the beginning of the seventeenth century. The basic idea is an extension of the original; an army would 'surround' a town or fortress much in the same way that a garment 'surrounds' the body.

JAR

Examples: a) He took a swig from the earthenware **jar**.
b) Her voice began to **jar** on my ears.
c) When we arrived the door was on the **jar**.

a) This is one of a number of words used in English that can trace their origins back to Arabic. The Arabic *jarrah* was originally a container for holding water, and as Arab culture and learning spread across Europe the word found its way into languages such as French (which has *jarre*), Spanish (which has *jarra* and *jarro*), and then eventually English. Interestingly, the pronunciation of the letter 'j' in English is similar to the French form of the word, but in Spanish it has retained the Arabic 'ch' sound (pronounced as in 'loch').

b) The origin of the word with this meaning is the Old English verb *ceorran* ('to creak'). Over time the word came to be associated with any loud, unpleasant noise or even the actions that could result in one. This meant that collisions, shaking, or unpleasant physical or mental shock could result in 'jarring'.

Another associated word is 'nightjar', a bird renowned for the raucous noise it has a habit of making during the night, 'jarring' on people's nerves and preventing them from sleeping.

c) A door which is said to be 'on the jar' (or, to use its more common equivalent, 'ajar') is slightly open and free to swing or turn on its hinges. It is derived from the Middle English expression *on char* ('on the turn').

But there is an interesting further development here. When the Old English derivative verb *cierre* evolved into the Middle English *char* it retained its meaning of 'turn' but had acquired the additional meanings of 'a turn of work' and 'a period of duty'. This explains why cleaning ladies, who would come in to work for perhaps an hour or two, used to be commonly referred to as 'charwomen'.

A parallel can be seen in modern English, which uses the Latin *rota* ('a wheel', i.e., something that 'turns') for a list of work to be done and personnel detailed to complete it.

JUNK

Examples: a) A solitary **junk** sailed into Hong Kong harbour.
b) The house was full of a load of old **junk**.

a) The term 'junk' for a sailing vessel has existed in English since about 1610 and was no doubt introduced by sailors and merchantmen opening the trade routes to the Far East. The immediate source for the English form of the word was the Portuguese _junco,_ a version of the Malay _jong_ and Javanese _djong._ The word is usually associated with the large, three-masted, flat-bottomed Chinese vessels so often seen in the East, particularly around the South China Sea.

b) The association between the word 'junk' and unwanted rubbish is also thought to be nautical in origin.

By the mid-fourteenth century the word was being used on board ships to designate old bits of rope or cable which served no purpose and were destined to be dumped at sea. It is believed that at least some of these ropes would have been of the type made from reeds or rushes, originally known in Latin as _iuncus_ (also spelled _juncus_) but anglicized as 'junk'. In the eighteenth century the old sailors found another use for the word. Meat taken on long voyages in those days was heavily salted and consequently very tough. The old sea dogs referred to it as 'junk' since it frequently tasted more like old rope than anything vaguely edible. The similarity to the expression 'junk food', however, is almost certainly coincidental as this term was first used in 1971.

Since 1923 'junk' has also been used in some quarters to refer to illegal drugs, and this has provided us of course with the noun for a user of narcotics, 'junkie'.

'Junk mail' was first used in 1954, no doubt in association with the general term for discarded or unwanted waste.

JUST

Examples: a) He was thought of as a **just** and honourable soldier.
b) Jane was **just** fifteen when her father died.

a) The idea of fairness and moral rectitude associated with the adjective 'just' is derived from the Latin _ius_ ('right' or 'legal right'; not to be confused with the homonym _ius_ meaning 'soup' or 'broth') and is cognate with the Sanskrit _yōs_ ('safety'). The implication here is that a 'just' society is more likely to guarantee security than an unjust one in which lawlessness might flourish.

By the fourteenth century the term was being applied to individuals who may or may not have had anything to do with the legal processes of a given society, but were simply considered to be equitable and trustworthy in their dealings with their fellow men.

It was also about this time that the word acquired a wider meaning of accuracy in non-legal contexts and was also used to emphasize precision in terms such as 'just right', 'just so', etc.

A derivative verb, *iustificare* ('to make just' or 'to act in a fair manner'), gave rise to another meaning; as printing developed, typesetters employed the verb to mean 'justify' or 'straighten out' a margin. The term first entered English in the 1670s and is still heard today in the expression 'right/left justification'.

The verb 'to adjust' is now used to mean 'to set right' and has every appearance of being related to concepts of justice and correctness, but this is historically incorrect. This verb is derived from the late Latin *adiuxtare* ('to place near to') from the Latin *ad* ('to') and *iuxta* ('near'). Presumably, objects set close to each other simply looked tidier than those scattered about in apparent disorder.

b) By the 1660s another development could be detected; 'just' had slipped from meaning 'exactly' to 'barely' or 'scarcely'. We can now describe something in English as being 'just right' (exactly as required) but also 'just in time' (barely on time).

KIND

Examples: a) 'What **kind** of man would say that?' she asked.

b) The **kind** young man helped her cross the busy road.

a) The modern English noun 'kind' is descended from the Old English *cynn*, which survives in the expressions 'next of kin' and 'kith and kin'. *Cynn* is derived from the Gothic *kuni* ('family'), directly cognate with the modern German *Kind* 'child'.

But *cynn* in Old English also meant 'race' or 'nature'; so when we ask what 'kind' of man a person is, we are really asking either what race he belongs to or what his nature is.

'Kith' (*cyth* in Old English) could refer to one's neighbours, fellow country-men, friends, or even to one's native land. Since the fourteenth century it has referred to relatives in general.

The Indo-European root behind all of these is **gen/*gon* ('to give birth' or 'to produce'), making 'kith', 'kin', and 'kind' cognate with Latin *gens* ('people', 'tribe', or 'nation') and the verb *gignere* ('to beget').

b) The use of the adjective 'kind' to mean affectionate or considerate is not unrelated to the noun, but the association has become somewhat blurred with the passage of time. In Anglo-Saxon times a person described as *cynn* would have behaved correctly (i.e., with sympathy and consideration to one's family, relatives, and loved ones). Eventually the meaning widened until by around the year 1300 anyone described as 'kind' would have been expected to behave in a benign and compassionate manner to one's fellow men in general and not solely to one's own family.

A similar evolution can be detected in another cognate word: 'generous'. If the Romans described somebody as *generosus*, it simply meant that that person was of noble birth, and this meaning persisted in English until the late sixteenth century. By the late seventeenth century, however, it had come to mean 'unself-ish', presumably because aristocrats were expected to behave in a compassionate manner, at least to those of equal social standing if not to the baser crowd.

LABOUR

Examples: a) The British **Labour** Party came into being around 1900.
            b) She went into **labour** on Christmas Eve.

a) The modern spelling of 'labour' is derived from the Latin *labor* ('hardship' or 'toil') and both terms are connected with the Latin verb *laborare* ('to work'). But the Latin *laborare* is probably allied to another verb, *labare* ('to totter under a heavy burden' or 'to be about to fall'), and interestingly, considering the number of countries that have adopted the term 'labour' for left-wing politicians and parties, *laborare* had the additional meaning in ancient Rome of 'to waver' or 'to be indecisive' (i.e., in politics). A further link is with the verb *labi* ('to slip' or 'to slide') and its associated noun, *lapsus*, as in the phrase *lapsus linguae* ('a slip of the tongue').

The demanding physical exertion associated with Latin *labor* can also be seen in modern French and Spanish, which have preserved much of the original sense. The principal meaning of *labourer* in the former and *laborar* in the latter is 'to plough' or 'to dig over' the land to make it suitable for planting the crops.

b) The use of the word to denote or describe the physical demands imposed on a woman during childbirth dates back to the 1590s. Prior to that, the Old French expression *en travail* (from the verb *travailler* ('to work')) had been used in English (since the thirteenth century). This verb and its Spanish counterpart, *trabajar*, are derived from the Latin *trepalium* (a compound noun made up of *tres* ('three') and *palus* ('stick')), an instrument with which slaves in ancient Rome were beaten in order to make them work harder. A further linguistic link is seen in the modern English 'travel', a reflection of just how arduous an undertaking a journey used to be in the days before cars, superfast trains, and international flight.

LAP

Examples: a) She held the baby in her **lap** while she fed him.
            b) The kitten began to **lap** up milk.

a) We now tend to think of the 'lap' as being the part of the body between the top of the leg and the knees when one is in a seated position, but it has only had this meaning since about 1300. The 'lap' (from the Indo-European root **leb* ('to hang')) was originally the loose, dangly piece of material that hung down from clothing, such as a shirt or blouse, worn on the upper body. The Old English word was *læppa*, cognate with both late Latin *lobus* ('husk' or 'pod') and the

Greek *lobos* meaning either a 'lobe' of the ear or a 'vegetable pod;' the common denominator here is the idea of 'hanging down'.

If we take things a stage further it is not difficult to see how the concept of a loose piece of material, dangling down and covering another, has provided English with another verb, 'to overlap'. This has also led to several figurative uses such as in 'his visit will overlap with mine' or in a sporting context when we use a shortened form of the verb and talk of one runner 'lapping' another.

b) When we turn to the other kind of 'lap' we uncover some very surprising associations. Old English had *lapian* ('to drink up') and this is directly associated with the modern German word for 'spoon', *Löffel*. The modern English, the German and Old English words are all cognate with the Latin *lambere* and the Greek *laptein*, both of which meant 'to lick'. And they are also probably linked to the Russian *lobzat'* ('to kiss').

LASH

Examples: a) He was told to **lash** the load down securely on the lorry.
b) She began to **lash** out at everyone in the room.
c) His wife had beautiful eyes with long **lashes**.

a) The use of the word 'lash' meaning 'to tie down' or 'to secure with ropes' is first recorded in the 1620s and is thought to have been a nautical term. Its immediate antecedent was the Middle French verb *lachier*, developed from the Old French *lacier* ('to lace'). This was derived from the Latin *laqueus*, a huntsman's term for a noose or snare and it associated verb *lacere* ('to lure' or 'to entice'). In the early thirteenth century the associated French word *laz* was applied to interwoven strands of silk, which developed into both 'lasso' and, by the 1550s, the delicate needlework patterns we now know as 'lace'. In other words, the word 'lash' brings together themes of binding, luring, and adornment.

b) When we talk of somebody 'lashing out' with their fists we are comparing their actions with that demonstrated not all that long ago when whipping was frequently used as a form of corporal punishment. Middle English had the word *lasche* for 'whip'.

c) The application of the word 'lashes' to the fine hairs growing out of the upper and lower eyelids is more difficult to explain. It could be their resemblance to the fine pieces of string used in lacemaking or perhaps the way they move rapidly up and down like a *lasche* or whip. A third possibility, remembering that the derivation of the word is associated with entrapment, is that they were originally perceived as part of a lady's armoury of flirtation techniques. The term 'eyelash' has been used in English since the eighteenth century.

Not unrelated to the powers of seduction is the word 'delicious'. This adjective is now virtually synonymous with 'tasty' but its derivation from the Latin *laqueus* reveals its original association with attraction, allurement, and entrapment.

LAST

Examples: a) Fred missed the **last** bus and had to walk home.

b) The money did not always **last** till the end of the month.

c) 'The cobbler should stick to his **last**' is an old proverb.

a) In Old English the word *læt* meant the same as our word 'late', and it had two superlatives: *latost* ('latest' as an adjective) and *lætest* ('latest' as an adverb). Both can be considered as the source of the modern English adjective and adverb 'last'.

The derivation of the Old English words is to be found in the Old Norse *latr* ('sluggish' or 'slow') and is cognate with the Latin *lassus* ('weary'). They all can be traced back to the Indo-European roots **lad* ('slow') and **le* ('to slacken'), seen also in modern English 'to let' (as in 'to let go').

b) 'To last' in the sense of 'to endure' or 'to survive' is derived from an Old English verb *læsten* ('to continue'), but it literally meant 'to follow a track', from the synonymous Proto-Germanic **laistjan*. And there is a very surprising link here. The root of **laistjan* is the Indo-European *leis* ('track' or 'furrow'), the same root that gave Old English the word *leornian*, the modern form of which is 'learn'. The explanation here appears to be that learning involves the acquisition of knowledge by following a defined course of instruction and 'tracking down' information.

c) Not unrelated to this concept is the cobbler's 'last', the block on which a shoe-maker fashions shoes. The Old English *læst* meant 'boot' and *lāst* meant 'foot-print' or 'the sole of the foot'. Both are allied to *leistr*, the Old Norse for 'foot'.

It is also interesting here to note the connection between the Scandinavian roots and their associated Latin words. The Old English *lāst* is directly related to the Latin *lira* ('furrow') and its derivative verb *delirare* ('to leave the furrow'). Over time this verb acquired a figurative usage suggesting deviation from the norm or even madness, as still seen in the English adjective 'delirious'.

LAY

Examples: a) She decided to **lay** the cat on the bed.
   b) A the age of 21 he became a **lay** preacher.
   c) Sir Walter Scott wrote 'The **Lay** of the Last Minstrel'.

a) 'Lay' meaning 'to put into a lying position' or 'to deposit on the ground' entered Middle English as *leyen* from the Germanic root **lag* ('to put'). This is also the origin of modern German *legen*, Dutch *leggen* and Danish *lægge*. The generic idea of depositing something on the ground is why we refer to hens 'laying' eggs when we actually mean 'producing' them.

A possibly surprising cognate is the word 'law'. This word is now understood as a rule or system of rules which members of a given society are expected to observe. Originally, however, it referred to orders and regulations which had been 'laid' down for the guidance of all.

b) Traditionally, societies have always been divided into two parts: those who were members of the clergy and those who were not. And those who were not were (and still are) referred to as the 'laity'. The word is derived from the late Latin *laicus* and ancient Greek *laikos*, both derived from the Greek *laos*, a noun with a variety of meanings: (i) the people, (ii) an army of men, (iii) foot soldiers (rather than those who serve at sea), and (iv) the ordinary citizens (as opposed to a society's leaders). In the plural, *laoi*, it specifically referred to the subjects of a prince.

An adjective which is possibly, but not definitely, connected with this word is 'lewd'. In Old English it was *læwede* and simply referred to the 'lay' or non-clerical section of the community. By the thirteenth century the adjective implied those lacking an education, and by the fourteenth it was associated with vulgarity and lasciviousness.

c) This one is a bit of a mystery. There are some etymologists who see 'lay' (a narrative poem, particularly one that has to be sung) as Celtic in origin and possibly related to the Old Irish *loid* or *laid* (modern Irish has *laoidh* or *laoi* for 'poem' and Scots Gaelic *laoidh*). Others see a connection with Gothic *liuthon* ('to sing') and modern German *Lied* ('song').

LEAN

Examples: a) He had to **lean** against the wall to steady himself.

b) Nigel was not skinny, but he was certainly **lean**.

a) The Old English verb *hlænian* and the Middle English *lenan* meant 'to place something in a leaning position', as does the modern English 'to lean'. The Indo-European root of the word 'lean' is **klin/*klein*, which also produced the Greek infinitive *klinein*, responsible for many other words in English and other languages. Two of the most unexpected cognates are 'clinic' and 'ladder'. The Greek *klinein* had a derivative noun *klinē*, originally anything against which one supported oneself, first of all in a standing position and later when lying down. In other words, *klinē* developed the additional meaning of 'bed'. By the nineteenth century this gave us the word 'clinic' for a specialized hospital; in the seventeenth century, however, a 'clinic' was a bedridden patient rather than the establishment in which the patient was treated. Another surprising relative here is the word 'climax;' this is a borrowing of the Greek word *klimax* simply meaning a 'ladder'.

From its spelling, a 'ladder' might not immediately appear connected with the verb 'to lean', but it is. The same Indo-European root, **klin*, produced *hleitara* in Old High German, Old English *hlædder*, and Middle English *lādder*. This eventually evolved into the form we have in modern English.

There has also been some discussion among linguists concerning the relationship with the word 'client'. Some authoritative dictionaries state that 'client' is derived from the Latin *cluere* ('to be called' or 'to hear oneself named'), but others claim that it is related to the Greek *klinein* ('to put in a leaning position'). The thinking here is that a 'client' was originally somebody who would 'lean' on somebody else for advice and protection. In English the first 'clients' were those who took advice from lawyers, but by the 1600s the term had acquired a more universal application.

b) 'Lean' as an adjective meaning 'sparse' or 'without fat or flesh' dates from the early thirteenth century, but its etymology seems unclear. Some authorities state that the origin is obscure, whereas others point to a connection with the verb. The thinking here was that bulk (whether of flesh or fat) suggested strength but a slender appearance was indicative of weakness and the inability to stand upright. There could be some basis for this theory in the related Old English verb *hlensian*, which meant both 'to cause to lean' and 'to weaken'.

LEFT

Examples: a) Jane could only write with her **left** hand.
   b) Unfortunately there is no apple pie **left**.

a) In many cultures the 'left' has been associated historically with any combination of misfortune, bad luck, and evil forces. Since the thirteenth century 'left' has been used in English as the opposite of 'right' (derived from Old English *riht* ('good'), cognate with the Latin *rectus* ('straight')) and was originally a Kentish dialect word, *lyft* ('weak' or 'foolish'). It supplanted the Old English *winestra* (literally 'friendlier'), a development due to the superstitious belief that if we refer to the left side euphemistically the evil forces residing there will be placated. Such attempts to assuage the dark forces of the left are also seen in the manner in which the Greeks and Romans dealt with the problem. The Greeks replaced *laios* ('left') with *aristeros* (derived from *aristos* ('the best')), meaning 'left' or 'boding ill'. Their augurs (i.e., fortune tellers who predicted the future after studying the flight of birds) faced north and experienced signs of evil or disaster approaching from the left. The Roman augurs, however, faced south and had the east (i.e., the 'lucky' quarter) on their left, and for them *laevus* meant 'fortunate', whereas for the rest of the population it meant 'left', 'silly', or 'unlucky'.

The other Latin word for 'left', *sinister*, also has an interesting history. It is thought to be associated with a Sanskrit word meaning 'more useful' even though its association with the left engendered interpretations of misfortune and bad luck. By contrast, for Roman fortune tellers the word still retained its meaning of 'fortunate' or 'favourable'. The associations of 'sinister' with evil and wrongdoing only became fixed in English in the fifteenth century.

b) As the past tense of 'to leave', the word 'left' has some very odd relatives. The Old English *læfan* meant 'to allow to remain' or 'not to take away'. In other words, the modern interpretation of 'to depart' reflects a shift of emphasis; originally, if we 'left' home we were not so much departing as acknowledging that the house would remain behind. Supporting evidence of this can be seen in the word's German cognate verb *bleiben* ('to remain').

The Indo-European root here is **leip* ('to stick' or 'to adhere to'; also the noun 'fat'), which makes the modern English verb cognate with the Greek words *lipos* ('grease'), *liparēs* ('persistent') and the verb *liparein* ('to stick to', 'to persist', or 'to persevere'). Presumably, the connection here is that persistence and adherence are closely related to concepts of remaining or being 'left behind' when others have departed.

LIE

Examples: a) He was told not to **lie** to his teacher again.

b) Jane loves to **lie** in bed with a good book.

a) The verb 'to lie' meaning to tell an untruth has existed in English since the twelfth century and its derivative noun (i.e., 'a lie') since the thirteenth. In Old English the word was *legen, ligan*, or, in an even older form, *leogan* and had a wider general meaning of 'to deceive' or 'to betray'. The Germanic root from which they were descended was **leugan*, from the Indo-European **leugh* ('to speak falsely').

A synonym for a wizard, 'warlock' is interesting here for the way in which it combines linguistic history with the concepts of deceit, betrayal, and truth. The Old English term was *wærloga*, a term the Anglo-Saxons used for a traitor, sorcerer, or wizard that was formed through a combination of *wær* (allied to the Latin *verax* ('speaking the truth')) and *loga* (Old English for 'liar'). This combination reflects the ancient belief that traitors, liars, magicians, and wizards shared a common talent: the ability to either lie or tell the truth depending on the situation.

Another word for the truth or reality in Anglo-Saxon times was *soð*, and its related noun *soðsagu* meant 'a true story'. This word evolved into the character so beloved of Shakespeare, the 'soothsayer', a seer who claimed to be able to foretell the future. It also gave us the verb 'to soothe', which originally meant 'to demonstrate the truth'. Later it acquired the meaning of 'to convince by flattery', but by the eighteenth century meant 'to calm somebody down' by persuading him or her that all was as it should be and that one had nothing to worry about.

b) The modern spelling 'to lie' has existed in English since the early part of the twelfth century. In Old English it was *licgan*, from the Indo-European root **legh* and the Proto-Germanic **legjan*. It is linked etymologically with the Latin *lectus* ('bed') and the Greek *lekhos* ('couch' or 'bed').

The Greek infinitive 'to lie', *koimasthai*, is responsible for a rather amusing linguistic coincidence in English. An associated transitive verb, *koimaein*, ('to put to sleep' or 'to lay down') also gave *koimētērion*, which we now use in English but spell as 'cemetery', the place where people are laid to rest for their final sleep. But the same verb produced *kōmē* ('village'; probably the origin of the English 'home') and *kōmos* 'village revelry'. This was then at some stage combined with another Greek word *ōdē* ('song' or English 'ode') to produce the modern English 'comedy'. In other words, 'cemetery' and 'comedy' are, linguistically speaking, very close relatives.

LIGHT

Examples: a) The bag was half empty and therefore very **light**.
           b) They walked along the river bank by the **light** of the moon.

a) The Proto-Germanic root **lingtaz* produced several cognate adjectives in the Germanic languages: Old Norse had *lettr,* Gothic had *leihts,* and modern German has *leicht.* Further afield, modern Russian has *lyogkiy,* an adjective which, in its plural form, is used as a noun equating to another cognate in English, 'lungs'. And the association between the English and Russian terms is further emphasized by the butchers' offerings in Britain known as 'offal and lights' (i.e., 'lungs').

The cognate adjective in Latin was *levis,* the source of several English derivatives including 'levitate', 'relieve', and 'alleviate'. The Latin adjective had an associated verb *levare* ('to lift' or 'to make light'), the origin of the Old French *levier* and modern English 'lever', a device for making weights easier to lift by making them seem 'lighter'.

Two Greek adjectives illustrate perfectly the association in the ancients' minds between things that are small and things that are light: *elakhus* ('small') and its cognate *elaphros* ('light'). But the link is perhaps best seen in Irish Gaelic. The word *lu* means 'smallest' but is cognate with 'light' and is at the root of the word *luchorpan.* This has been anglicized into the 'small' (and therefore light) people from Irish mythology whom we now know as 'leprechauns'.

A closely associated verb is 'to alight'. We can now talk about alighting from any vehicle, but originally the idea was that 'alighting' from a horse would make its burden 'lighter'.

b) 'Light' (as opposed to darkness) is derived from the Indo-European **leuk* and the Proto-Germanic **leukhtem* ('brightness'). In Old English the word was *leoht* and later *leht,* cognates of the Greek *leukos* ('white'; as in the medical term 'leukaemia', literally meaning 'white blood') and the Latin *lux* ('light').

Whereas the Greek for 'white' is related to the English adjective 'light', the Greek for the noun 'light' was *phōs,* which has provided English with words such as 'photograph' (written in light) and 'phosphorus' (bringer of light). And when *phosphorus* (*phosphoros* in Greek) is translated into Latin the result is *lucifer* also 'bringer of light'.

LIST

Examples: a) She made a **list** of the things she needed.
b) Suddenly the ship began to **list** to starboard.
c) The **lists** were once a popular form of entertainment.

a) The clue to the origin of this usage of the word lies in the fact that 'lists' tend to be written in columns; in Old High German and Old Norse the word *līsta* meant the border or hem of a piece of cloth. In the interests of economy these were sometimes torn off to make smaller articles of clothing (e.g., 'list slippers') and at some point somebody presumably realized that the same strips of material were convenient for making notes or 'lists' of things to do or articles to buy. This use of the word in English dates from the early seventeenth century.

b) A ship listing to one side or the other has its etymological roots in a now archaic use of the word meaning 'to please', as in the King James Version of the Bible where we read, 'The wind bloweth where it listeth' (John iii. 8). This 'list' was written *lystan* in Old English and was related to the modern English word 'lust' but generally meant 'a wish to' or 'a desire to', unlike the modern usage of the word with its narrow sexual connotations. In other words, a ship that 'lists' to starboard can be thought of as 'willing' or 'wishing' to do so, much the same way that we can talk about a person being 'inclined' to a certain course of action.

The same word also occurs in the adjective 'listless', said of someone who lacks the 'will' to do anything.

c) The medieval form of mass entertainment involving knights in shining armour charging at each other at breakneck speed can be referred to either as 'the joust' or 'the lists' (always plural). The explanation for this is allied to usage (a) above since these battles royal tended to be confined to the outer limits of a field where perhaps a market or fair was in progress.

To complete the picture, it might be added that the word 'joust' is ultimately derived from the Latin *iuxta* ('together'), as the event was basically a contest in which knights and horses 'came together' to take part in sporting (and possibly mortal) combat.

LITTER

Examples: a) The sow produced a larger **litter** than was expected.

b) The children were taught not to throw **litter** in the street.

a) It might seem surprising, but both uses of the word 'litter' in modern English can trace their history back to an original idea of lying on a bed. In Middle English the word was *litere*, adopted from the Old French for a portable bed, stretcher, or bier, *litiere*. The word survives in Modern French *lit*, the normal word for any kind of bed. All these words, together with the equivalent Latin *lectus* and Greek *lektron*, were descended from the Indo-European root **lagh/*legh*, the origin of English words such as 'to lie', 'to lay', and even 'lair'. It is also the root which has produced the word 'lager', which in German means 'a camp' or 'storeroom' but in English is a beer that has been kept 'lying' in store for some time.

b) The connection with abandoned rubbish is rather tortuous. In former times those who tended farm and domestic animals saw it as part of their duties to provide reasonably comfortable conditions for their animals when they were about to give birth. This involved spreading straw on the ground to create a bed for the new piglets, calves, etc. The bed, or *litere*, eventually expanded in meaning to include the young animals as well as the straw or old bits of cloth which provided their first contact with the world.

As the straw, odd bits of material, etc., were more often than not just flung on the floor in no particular order, it was not long before the meaning shifted from the specialized to the general. By the eighteenth century, a 'litter' was no longer just a makeshift bed or group of very young animals; it had acquired the additional meaning we attribute to it today, i.e., 'discarded waste'.

LOOM

Examples: a) She sat at the **loom** from dawn till dusk.

b) Suddenly the ship began to **loom** out of the fog.

a) There is some discussion among linguists as to the origin of this word, but most seem to agree that the machine designed for making cloth is derived from the Old English *geloma* and Middle English *lōma*, both of which simply meant 'tool', 'instrument', or 'utensil'. There is also a possible link with the Old High German word *lōdo* ('coarse cloth'). Considering the inherent association between a loom and cloth, this is a distinct possibility.

Where there seems to be no doubt is in the word's association with another English word, 'heirloom'. This entered English early in the fifteenth century and is a combination of 'loom' and 'heir' (from the Latin *heres*). 'Loom' by this time had acquired the more general meaning of 'property'.

b) Dating from the late sixteenth century, the use of the word 'loom' to mean something (usually of considerable size) gradually coming into view is thought to be Scandinavian in origin. Swedish has *loma* and East Frisian has *lomen*, both of which mean 'to move slowly'. The etymologist Walter Skeat connects the word with Middle English *lumen* ('to shine'; from the Latin *lumen* ('light')) and suggests that the basic idea is of objects previously hidden from view suddenly becoming visible because of their luminosity or brilliance. There may also be a connection with the word 'lame' as lameness in a human or animal can result in slowness of movement.

LOT

Examples: a) It fell to his **lot** never to marry.

b) It was decided to draw **lots** for the money.

c) He doesn't eat a **lot** for a man of his size.

d) At the auction she bid for **lot** 21.

a) The modern spelling of the word is derived from the Old English *hlot* meaning 'a portion' or 'a share'. It was also the term for any object used in decision-making processes based on the practice of 'drawing lots' and the inevitable association here with ideas of chance or destiny is reflected in the modern German cognate noun *Los* ('fate').

b) In situations where people would prefer not to be responsible for making a decision which might prove unpopular a frequent course of action is to 'draw lots'. The Old English verb here is *hleotan*, but the Gothic word *hlauts* ('inheritance'), a close linguistic relative, is a clue to the ancient practice of drawing lots to decide how a man's property would be divided up among surviving relatives after his death. Interestingly, our words 'clergy' and 'clergyman' share a similar origin; the Greek *klēros*, from the verb *klan* ('to break off'), meant 'inheritance' or 'priestly order' but originally referred to the pieces of pottery 'broken off' and thrown into a bag before the selection process began. The ecclesiastical connection stems from the conviction that a gentleman of the cloth's 'inheritance' is to devote his life to the service of God.

c) The notion of 'lot' meaning 'a considerable amount of' is a relatively modern one. Presumably it is associated with the assumption or hope that any 'portion' of an endowment or inheritance would always be large.

d) The use of the word in auctions has evolved with time. It reflects how, originally, articles for sale at auction were household articles and personal belongings 'inherited' from recently departed parents or more distant forebears.

Other related words which have found their way into modern English include 'lottery', 'lotto', and 'allotments' (parcels of land which were originally awarded or granted to people in the sixteenth century). Once again there is an interesting parallel here with Greek. The Greek verb *nemein* ('to distribute' or 'to allot') had a related noun *nomós* ('pasture land allotted to a tribe'). And the tribesmen who wandered around such pastures with their grazing flocks were *nomades*, or, as we would now refer to them, 'nomads'.

MAGAZINE

Examples: a) There was only one round left in the rifle's **magazine**.
b) She bought the **magazine** to read on the train.

a) The word 'magazine' was in common use in English in the late sixteenth century and referred to a storehouse, usually for armaments and ammunition. The word was first applied to the chamber containing the bullets on a Spencer repeating rifle during the American Civil War and has been the usual term for such an attachment ever since.

The English borrowed the word from the French, who had been using *magasin* (borrowed from the Italian *magazzino*) since the fifteenth century to denote any place where belongings or equipment could be stored. But the ultimate source of the word was the Arabic *makhzan* ('storehouse'), a derivative of the verb *khazana* ('to store up'). The word is also the origin of the modern French *magasin* ('shop') and the Spanish *almacén* ('warehouse' or 'department store').

Other Arabic words that made their way into modern English include *kahwa* ('coffee'), *suffa* ('sofa'), *sharbat* ('sherbet'), and *'attabi* ('tabby').

b) In 1731 a journal called *The Gentleman's Magazine* was first published in London under the editorship of Edward Cave. It was a collection of stories and articles which, it was hoped, would appeal to the educated classes and provide them with sufficient quantity and variety of reading matter to occupy their leisure time until the next edition appeared. Such a collection of articles obviously bore analogy to storehouses or warehouses and so the term 'magazine' seemed appropriate.

Other terms denoting various types of printed matter entered English about this time. 'Gazette' appeared around 1600, taking its name from the Italian news-sheet which sold for a *gazeta*, a coin of very little value that bore the image of a *gazza* (Italian for 'magpie'). 'Journals', from the French *jour* ('day'), began to appear in 1728 and, as the name suggests, were daily publications, but 'periodicals' (first use of the term thought to be 1798) were intended to appear at irregular intervals.

MAIL

Examples: a) He sent the letter by first-class **mail**.
           b) Chain **mail** formed part of a medieval knight's armour.

a) The association of the word 'mail' with the delivery of letters and parcels is a relatively modern one, but its linguistic antecedents offer an explanation of how the connection evolved. The basic idea of a postman walking around town carrying a bag of some description and pushing letters through specially designed slots in front doors has probably not changed much over the years. The main difference is that we now refer to the articles being delivered as 'mail' whereas until the seventeenth century the word was applied to the bag rather than its contents. If we go back further in time, we find an even earlier connection. In ancient Greek the word *molgos* referred to the animal hide that commonly provided the material from which bags of varying types and sizes were made. The name of the material was eventually applied to the end product itself; thus the Old High German *malaha* meant 'bag' or 'pouch'. The same word found its way into Old French, which had *male* for 'wallet', and modern French, which still retains *malle* for 'trunk' or 'valise'. In modern Irish and Scots Gaelic the words for 'bag' are *mála* and *màla* respectively.

What we refer to as 'blackmail' has nothing to do with the mail. It has its origins in sixteenth-century Scotland, where the clan chieftains would meet up on a regular basis and agree how much payment they were going to demand from the peasant farmers. The term used for this agreement was the Old Norse and Old English *mal*, which combined with the word 'black' (with all its negative connotations) gave us the word as we understand it today.

b) Chain mail took its name from the Latin *macula* ('spot') as the little holes in a chain mail garment produced a dappled or 'spotted' effect on the skin of the wearer. This is the same Latin word that gave us 'mackerel', a fish known for its mottled skin, and 'immaculate', meaning 'unblemished', 'perfect', or, quite literally, 'without spots'.

MANDARIN

Examples: a) He was one of the **mandarins** of Whitehall.

b) She is fluent in Japanese and **Mandarin**.

c) The **mandarin** is closely related to the tangerine.

a) It is generally accepted that the first Europeans to refer to Chinese adminis-trators as 'mandarins' were the Portuguese who encountered oriental official-dom when the trade routes to China opened up in the sixteenth century. The Portuguese traders acquired the Malay term *mantra*, derived from the Sanskrit *mantrin* ('counsellor'). Interestingly, *mantrin* is derived from the Sanskrit *mantiš* ('thought') and is cognate with Latin *mens*, the word which gave English such words as 'mind' and 'mental'. The Sanskrit word also produced 'mantra', now used to denote any frequently repeated phrase but in Buddhism and Hinduism a sound designed specifically to induce concentration and a deeply meditative state of mind. It would be easy to conclude that the Portuguese associated the ability to think with high office, but the more likely explanation is that they confused it with their own verb *mandar* ('to give orders' or 'to command') and so referred to any Chinese official in a position of authority as a *mandarim*.

The first use of the word as an unofficial, semi-jocular term for a government official or senior civil servant in Britain dates from 1907.

b) English speakers now refer to the official language of mainland China as Mandarin, but the Chinese call their language *putonghua*, which literally means 'the common language'. The explanation here is quite simple: Western traders visiting China in the early seventeenth century referred to the strange new tongue they encountered as the 'mandarim language' (i.e., 'the language of the administrators') and this was eventually simplified with a change of spelling to 'Mandarin'.

c) The small, sweet-tasting fruit we know as 'mandarins' or 'mandarin oranges' also have the oriental officials to thank for their name. When the eighteenth-century traders first brought them back from China, the colour of the fruit's skin reminded the importers of the yellow robes traditionally worn by Chinese figures of authority. But 'mandarins' (or at least a closely related fruit) were also grown in North Africa and these were known as the 'fruit of Tangiers' or, in their more recognizable form, 'tangerines'.

MAROON

Examples: a) She chose the **maroon** dress for the party.
           b) They decided to **maroon** the captain on a remote island.
           c) The sailors fired a **maroon** to signal their position.

a) Maroon as an adjective used to describe a colour somewhere between brown and crimson entered English from other European languages which have the nouns *marron* (French), *marrone* (Italian), and *marrón* (Spanish) for what we know in English as a chestnut. And all of these can trace their origins back to the Greek *maraon* or *maraos*, the fruit of the cornel tree, otherwise known in English as the dogwood tree and renowned for its very hard wood.

b) Anybody who has ever read of the swashbuckling adventures of eighteenth-century pirates on the Spanish Main will have heard about the fate of many a sailor who fell foul of the captain, or many a captain who fell foul of a mutinous crew. Inevitably their fate was to find themselves 'marooned' on a desert island. This use of the word found its way into English from the Spanish *cimarrón* ('wild' or 'untamed'), no doubt a fitting description for the surroundings anyone aban-doned on a desert island might find.

Historically, the Spanish word was applied to a particular group of people: runaway slaves who were known collectively as *negros cimarrones* ('wild black men'). In South American Spanish, even today, the term *marrón* is a derogatory term for the descendant of a runaway slave.

Ultimately, the Spanish word *cimarrón* is derived from *cima* ('mountain peak'). The reasoning here appears to be that the wildest part of any desert island is the top of its tallest mountain.

c) There is some disagreement over the use of the term to denote a firework. Some etymologists are of the opinion that it is a reference to the shape, which they argue is similar to that of a chestnut. Others maintain that it is simply an extension of the use of the word to denote those who had found themselves, either by accident or design, stranded on a desert island. If this is the case, it could simply be an abbreviation of the terms 'maroon firework' or 'maroon rocket'.

MATCH

Examples: a) She was looking for a **match** for her expensive vase.
          b) He struck a **match** and lit the fire.

a) The basic idea behind matching one object with another or one person with somebody else is suitability. The Indo-European root at play here is **mak* ('to fit'), which is also the root behind the modern English verb 'to make'. The Old English *(ge)mæcca* meant 'mate' or 'one of a pair', a concept that can be seen in most of the English usages of the word; a 'matchmaker' is a person tasked with finding suitable marriage partners; articles of clothing are said to 'match' if they sit well together; and if one sportsman is described as a 'match' for another, the implication is that the two contestants are of similar strength and skill. By the 1540s games and sporting contests in which adversaries or competing sides squared up to each other in an attempt to demonstrate who was the strongest, fastest, or most skilful were being referred to as 'matches'.

b) The 'match' used in lighting fires has quite a convoluted history. Middle English had the word *macche*, which came from Old French *meiche* (modern French still has *mèche*), but all these words referred to the wick of an oil lamp or candle. They were all related to the Late Latin *myxa*, the little hole or nozzle in an oil lamp through which the wick protruded, and this in turn is thought to be derived from the Greek *muxa*. The Greek noun had several meanings: (i) the nozzle of a lamp, (ii) mucus, (iii) nostril, and (iv) the slime trail left by a snail. To the Greek mind, a 'wick' poking out of a lamp looked remarkably similar to 'snot' (from the Old English *gesnot* ('nasal mucus') and related to the word 'snout') exiting from a person's nostril and sliding down his upper lip. The use of the word 'match' to define a small piece of wood used for transferring a flame from a fire to a candle dates from the sixteenth century.

MATE

Examples: a) Pete went with his **mate** to the football match.
          b) Deer **mate** during the rutting season.
          c) He was first **mate** on a merchant ship.
          d) 'Check**mate!**' exclaimed his opponent.

a) The use of the word 'mate' as a synonym for 'friend' or as a form of address among workers, sailors, etc., has existed since the fifteenth century, and it is still common today in Britain. Its origin is thought to be found in Old High German, which had *gi-mazzo* ('someone with whom we eat'; from the Gothic *mats* ('food') and its associated verb *matjan* ('to eat')). There is a distinct parallel here with another commonly used noun, 'companion'. This is derived from the Latin *cum* ('with') and *panis* ('bread'), and thus the real meaning of the word was 'someone with whom we eat bread'. Russian has an interesting variant of this theme: *sobutyl'nik* (from *so* ('with') and *butyl'* ('a large bottle')) defines someone with whom we 'share a bottle', no doubt of something alcoholic.

The Gothic *mats* survives in modern Swedish and Danish, which both have *mad* for 'food'. In Anglo-Saxon it showed up as *mete*, the modern English 'meat', originally a term applied to any food, not just that derived from animal flesh; this explains the term 'sweetmeat' for cakes and other delicacies.

b) 'To mate' as animals do when they are selecting a male or female of the species in order to produce young is linguistically associated with the verb 'to match'. In other words, it is really a reference to the process of selection and pairing animals which appear to have the best chance of producing strong, healthy offspring.

c) The term 'shipmate' used as a generic term for a fellow sailor has been around since the first half of the eighteenth century. 'Mate' has been used with the more specific designation of deck officer on a merchant ship since the fifteenth century.

d) There is some discussion here about the origin of the term as used in the game of chess. The most authoritative sources claim that the term is ultimately from the Old Persian or Arabic *shah mat* meaning 'the king is dead'.

MAY

Examples: a) '**May** we come and see you?' asked the girls.
       b) She was born just before the end of **May**.
       c) The **May**flower set sail to the New World in 1620.
       d) A **May**day signal was sent just before the plane crashed.

a) The verb 'may' exists only in the present tense. It has no future tense, no past and no infinitive. The original past tense was 'might' but the two words have become so confused over time that 'might' is now frequently, if incorrectly, used as an alternative to 'may'. The Old English *mæg* meant 'am able' and had an infinitive form *magan*, both of which were derived from the Proto-Germanic root **mag* ('to have the power to') and Indo-European root **magh* ('to be able'). It exists in slightly varying forms in all the Germanic languages and is cognate with the Russian *mogu* ('I am able' and the noun *moshch'* 'power'). And a further cognate is the ancient Greek *mēkhos* ('means' or 'contrivance', i.e., a device for providing men with the strength or power to complete tasks which otherwise would have been beyond their capabilities. And this is the origin of all things 'mechanical' in English.

b) We know from the Venerable Bede's *On the Reckoning of Time*, written in AD 725, that the Anglo-Saxons had some wonderfully bucolic names for the seasons and months before they accepted Christianity. The fifth month they called *ðrim-ilcemonað* (literally 'three-milkings month') as it was the one month of the year when the cows could be milked three times per day.

'May' (introduced into England in the twelfth century) was derived from the Old French *mai*, which in turn came from the Latin *Maius*, so called by the Romans in honour of Maia, an earth goddess and wife of Vulcan. In Greek mythology, on the other hand, Maia, the daughter of Atlas and Pleionē, went on to be the mother of Hermes. In both cases, the Indo-European root for the name is **mag-ya* ('she who is great') and so is cognate with the Old Persian *Magi* 'the great ones') who are said to have attended the birth of Jesus.

c) The ship on which the Pilgrim Fathers sailed to America in the seventeenth century took its name from 'may', a sixteenth-century term for the blossoms of the hawthorn bush.

d) The international distress signal in use since 1923 is reputed to be derived from an abbreviated form of the French plea for help, *Venez m'aider!* ('Come and help me!').

MEAD

Examples: a) **Mead** is a powerful drink seldom heard of nowadays.

b) **Mead** appears in many place names in England.

a) In Saxon times and the Middle Ages mead was a much-quaffed alcoholic beverage made from water and fermented honey. In Old English it was spelled *meodu* and later, by the time of Middle English, it had become *mede*. Whatever the spelling, the word is cognate with Greek *methu* ('wine') and related to the Latin *merum* ('undiluted wine'). All these words are related to the Sanskrit *madhu* ('sweet') and are cognate with the modern Russian *myod* ('honey').

An almost unbelievable relative is the word we now think of as a precious stone, the 'amethyst'. The name is derived from the Greek *amethustos* ('a remedy against drunkenness'), the connection being that the ancient Greeks thought that wearing one or two of these stones around the neck was the perfect antidote to the intoxicating properties of *methu*. Another derivative noun is 'methyl', a combination of the Greek words *methu* and *hulē* ('wood' or 'forest'), coined originally to highlight the arboreal origins of this kind of alcohol.

b) For the origins of 'mead' as found in many place names (e.g., Broadmead, King's Mead, and Runnymede, which retains the Middle English spelling) we have to refer once again to the classical languages. In ancient Greek the verb *amaō* meant 'I reap', and was cognate with the Latin *metere* ('to reap' or 'to harvest'). These roots found their way into Old English with *māwan* and Middle English with *mōwen* ('to mow') and the derivative noun *mēd* ('meadow'). In other words, a 'meadow' (which we now tend to think of as an untended field) was originally a field as it appeared after it had been mown to provide hay.

Another related word which is quite commonly used figuratively in English is 'aftermath'. We tend to use it to refer to the results of some catastrophic event such as rioting, revolution, or war. The original Old English word *aftermaeth*, however, referred simply to what remained after the mowing had been completed.

MEDIC

Examples: a) The **medic** dashed over the road to help the injured man.
          b) The **medic** plant grows profusely throughout Europe.

a) The term 'medicine' defining the healing arts has been a feature of English since around the year 1200, but it was not applied to the potions and lotions given to the sick and the dying until the middle of the fourteenth century. The derivation of both was the Latin *medicina* ('the art of curing') and its associated noun *medicus* ('doctor').

The verb from which these terms were derived was *mederi* ('to cure'), but there is a fascinating and illuminating history behind this word. Its Indo-European root is *med ('to measure', 'to consider', 'to take appropriate action'; the same root has given us words such as 'metre', 'modicum', 'moderate', and 'modest'). A further linguistic relation is the Greek *medesthai* ('to plan for' or 'to ponder carefully'). It would appear, therefore, that the original professional 'medicine men' were mainly practitioners skilled in assessing a situation calmly before deciding what needed to be done.

It is also possible that these early medics would have been trained to know just how much medicine to 'measure out' for their patients. If so, there is an interesting parallel with the word 'chemistry', which is derived from the Greek word *khein* ('to pour').

The alternative word used in English to denote a dispenser of medical compounds is 'doctor', derived from the Latin *doctus*, which in turn comes from the verb *docere* ('to teach'). In other words, a 'doctor' was originally simply someone who 'had been taught'.

b) The plant known as 'medic' (alternatively spelled 'medick') belongs to the genus known as *Medicago* and is also known as 'alfalfa'. It has nothing to do with the word 'medicine' but takes its name ultimately from the Greek *Mēdikē poa* ('grass from Media'). Media was a country in Asia Minor situated roughly where modern Turkey borders north-western Iran.

MINT

Examples: a) She always makes **mint** sauce to have with lamb.
           b) He got a job in the Royal **Mint**.

a) Mint as a delicate herb used in cooking takes its name from ancient Greek *minthē*. This passed into other languages such as Latin, where it changed its form to *menta* or *mentha* (which shows up in the English word 'menthol'). The strange thing about the Greek word is that it can also have the form *minthos,* and this can be either a masculine or feminine noun. When it is grammatically feminine, it refers to the aromatic herb, but when masculine it means 'human excrement'. Exactly what the connection is, if there be one, is not clear.

The term 'spearmint' is derived from the Latin *mentha spicata* (literally 'spiked mint') and is so called because of its pointed leaves.

b) When used to designate the place where money is produced the origin of the word is equally fascinating, if rather complex. In this context 'mint' can be traced back to the Roman goddess Juno. She was the female equivalent of Jupiter and as such considered to be the queen of heaven. But she was also the guardian of finances and in this role was known as Juno Moneta (literally 'Juno the Advisor' or 'Juno who warns'; from the Latin verb *monere* ('to warn')).

The Romans built a temple to Juno on the Capitoline Hill, and within its grounds they also established a factory where money was to be coined. The association between Juno Moneta and coinage therefore was fixed and the epithet Moneta became the source of words such as 'mint' and 'money' in English. It was also the derivation of recognizably related words in other languages: French has *monnaie* for 'currency' or 'loose change'; Spanish and German have *moneda* and *Münze* respectively for 'coin'.

The use of the word 'mint' in English for the place where money is produced, dates from the fifteenth century.

Other words in modern English are derived from the same Latin verb *monere*. These include the verb 'to admonish' and the noun 'monster', which originally was just something people had to be 'warned' about.

MOOR

Examples: a) He loved to wander over the **moor** near his home.
b) Jim was told to **moor** the little boat securely.
c) Othello is described as the **Moor** of Venice.

a) The linguistic evidence suggests that this word has changed considerably over the centuries. We now think of a 'moor' as empty wasteland, perhaps with a fair covering of heather and shrubs, but its related nouns in other languages suggest that this type of terrain must have once been very wet. In Old English the word *mor* ('swamp') was related to the Old High German *muor* ('marsh', 'pool', or even 'sea'). Other cognates are Latin *mare*, Russian *morye*, and German *Meer* (all of which mean 'sea'), as well as modern German *Moor* ('bog'). It has also been suggested that these words may be related to the Sanskrit *maru* ('desert') and the verb *mrí* ('to die'). The implication here is that moorland, deserts, and even seas appeared to primitive man to be totally lifeless expanses.

b) This meaning of the word did not exist in Old or Middle English and only made its appearance towards the end of the fifteenth century. This no doubt was due to Dutch influence, as the word is a direct borrowing from *meren* ('to moor a boat'; in an older form, *merren*), a relative of the English 'to mar'. This now tends to mean 'to spoil' but it was also 'to hinder' or 'to impede', which would fit in with the idea of mooring or securing a boat to a riverbank and thus 'impeding' its movement.

c) Loosely, the term Moor used to apply to almost any dark-skinned inhabitant of North Africa, particularly areas close to modern Morocco. English adopted the term in the late fourteenth century, but it had been known in other parts of Europe long before that. In medieval Latin the term was *Morus* and in classical Latin *Mauros*, and both versions were taken from the ancient Greek *amauros* ('dark') and the later Greek *mauros* ('black').

MUST

Examples: a) I **must** finish this work by tonight.

b) 'There's a **musty** smell in here,' she said.

c) New wine is known as **must**.

d) Bull elephants are aggressive during **must**.

a) This verb has had an unusual history. It now only exists in the present tense but was originally the past tense of the Old English *mūt* or *mōt* ('may' or 'must'). Curiously, if the past tense of the verb is needed, a totally unrelated verb or phrase has to be used such as 'I had to'. Modern cognate verbs can be seen in the German *müssen* and the Dutch *moeten*. It is also thought that there is a link with the Indo-European root **med* ('to measure'), which suggests that the words 'medicine' and 'medicinal' are other relatives. The reasoning here could be that 'medicine' involves assessing what 'must' be done and what appropriate 'measures' need to be taken.

The use of the past tense with a present tense meaning dates from about 1300.

b) The adjective 'musty' is derived from the noun 'must' meaning mould and is almost certainly related to the word 'moist'. Its etymology is not very clear, but there is a strong possibility that it is connected with the Provençal *mousti/musti* ('damp' or 'humid'). If this is the case, the explanation probably lies in the link with (c).

c) 'Must' as a noun referring to new, unfermented wine is directly descended from the Latin *mustum*, an abbreviated form of *vinum mustum* ('fresh wine'). The Latin word is derived ultimately from the Indo-European root **meus* ('damp'), which has also given us the word 'moss'.

The word 'mustard' is also a close relative. This culinary delicacy has its origins in the Romans' practice of grinding the seeds of the *Sinapis* plant (now called the 'mustard plant' in English) into a powder and adding a few drops of new wine or *mustum* to form a smooth paste. The Romans' term for this was *mustum ardens* ('burning-hot fresh wine'), which evolved into the word we recognize today as 'mustard'. It was first recorded in English in the thirteenth century.

d) During the rutting season elephants and camels are said to be 'in must' (alternatively spelled 'musth'). This word has been in English since 1871 during the time of the British Raj in India. It entered the language from Persian (via Urdu) which has *mast* for 'drunk' or 'intoxicated'.

NAVE

Examples: a) The congregation crowded into the **nave**.

b) The **nave** was too small for the new axle.

a) Since about 1670 the main body of a church has been referred to in English as the 'nave'. The explanation here is that at some point it was noticed that the design of the central part of a church could easily remind a spectator of an upturned boat, the Latin for which is *navis*.

The Indo-European root here is **nau* ('boat' or 'voyage'), which has given modern English words such as 'navy', 'nautical', 'navigate', and 'navigator'. It has also given us the word 'navvy', now used colloquially for a manual labourer employed to dig up roads but originally a workman tasked with digging canals along which barges and boats could be 'navigated'.

b) The technical term 'nave' is the hub of a wheel (i.e., the hole at its centre through which the axle passes). In Old English it was referred to as the *nafu*, *nafa*, or *nabula*, from the Indo-European root **(n)obh*, closely linked to the Sanskrit *nabhih*, the Greek *omphalos*, and the Latin *umbilicus*, recognizable in the English adjective 'umbilical'. And the Greek *omphalos*, along with its Latin cognate *umbo*, was the term for the 'boss' on a shield.

Both *omphalos* and *umbo* were associated by the ancients with the centre of almost anything. The Greeks, for instance, referred to the centre of the island of Ogygia as *omphalos thalassēs* ('centre of the sea'), and Delphi, the home of the famous oracle, was also defined as an *omphalos* as it was believed to be the centre of the earth. The perceived association with the centre of an object explains the etymological connections between the Latin, Greek, and Sanskrit words and the modern English noun 'navel'.

NET

Examples: a) He went fishing but forgot to take his **net**.

b) Her **net** salary was hardly enough to live on.

a) The basic meaning of the word 'net' implies that a material of some sort has been bound, twisted, or knotted and transformed into a particular artefact. A 'fishing net', 'net curtains', a 'railway network' system, and even the second syllable in the word 'connection' can all trace their origin back to the Latin verb *nectere* ('to bind') and the Indo-European root **ned* with its strong associations with binding, knotting, and twisting. Old English had *nett*, which was the term for any net used for fishing or hunting but was also a common term for a spider's web. And figuratively, clouds drifting through the sky in close formation were also referred to as a *nett*.

It is also directly linked to the Latin *nodus*, which has provided the English words 'node' and 'nodule'.

b) 'Net' is frequently used in financial circles as the opposite of 'gross' to define what remains after taxes, expenditure, etc., have been deducted. The expression is closely related to the word 'neat', a derivative of the Latin *nitidus* ('bright'; from the verb *nitere* ('to shine')) and related to the modern French *net* ('clean').

But the Latin verb had an additional meaning of 'to glow with health' as two thousand years ago the Romans realized that the human body looked trimmer, fitter, and much healthier without accumulations of excess fat. Later on, the derivative 'neat' (and eventually 'net') came to be associated in English with just about anything from which all but the essentials had been removed; a room, for instance, stripped of unnecessary clutter, has been described as 'neat and tidy' since the sixteenth century. The etymology also explains why alcoholic drinks (particularly gin or whisky) taken without anything else added have been described since the early nineteenth century as 'neat'.

And there is another, less common use of the word 'neat'. It is now considered archaic, but it was historically a term applied to oxen as distinct from sheep and cows. The origin of this meaning is the Old English *neotan* ('to use'), which provides us with a reliable indication that the Anglo-Saxons regarded oxen as being of considerable practical use. They could, after all, be put to work in the fields, whereas sheep and cows did little else apart from provide food.

NURSERY

Examples: a) All the children slept in the **nursery**.

b) He looked after all the plants in the **nursery**.

a) The Old French verb *norrir* meant 'to provide for', 'to foster', or 'to maintain'. It was derived from the Latin *nutrire* ('to nourish' or 'to suckle'), which has a totally unexpected linguistic history; its origins are thought to lie in the Indo-European root *(s)nau* ('to swim'). There seems to be little, if any, connection between 'swimming' and 'nourishing' until we consider that a secondary meaning of the Indo-European root was 'to let flow'. This now offers a distinctly possible explanation which is supported by the cognate Sanskrit word *snauti* ('she gives milk').

The designation of 'nursery' for a special room set aside for the purpose of breastfeeding infants dates from around 1300, and 'nursery' designating a school for very young children dates from the late sixteenth century.

b) The first time someone had the idea of using the term 'nursery' for cultivating plants was in the 1560s. No doubt it suddenly occurred to him or her that plants and children are not all that dissimilar in that they both need to be well fed, cared for, and protected if they are to grow up strong and healthy and reach their full potential. But things did not stop there. Other thinkers spotted the connection, and over the years additional botanical expressions acquired a pedagogical application. A seminar, from the Latin *semen* ('seed') and originally simply a place where seeds were sown, took on the meaning of a group of students working under the guidance of a professor. Somewhat earlier, in the 1580s, the term 'seminary' (from the same Latin word) was used to define schools for training priests.

In 1840 the German educationalist Friedrich Fröbel (1782–1852) developed the concept of treating young children as delicate plants and coined the expression *Kindergarten* ('children's garden'). The term was adopted universally and applied to educational establishments where the very young could be nurtured and guided in the hope that they would blossom into fine examples of their kind.

ORDER

Examples: a) All his books are arranged in alphabetical **order**.
b) She gave up her job and joined a religious **order**.
c) The officer gave the **order** to advance.
d) Max went into town to **order** a new coat.

a) There is a strong possibility that all the meanings attached to the word 'order' are derived from the age-old occupation of weaving. All the usages of the associated Latin noun *ordo* imply people or articles arranged in a straight line. These include: (i) a series, line, or row; (ii) a row of seats in a theatre; (iii) banks of oars on a vessel; and (iv) a line of soldiers. The underlying idea of a coherent arrangement is contained in the related verb *ordiri* ('to begin to weave a web' or 'to lay the warp'). The prehistoric origin here is probably the Proto-Italic **ored* ('to arrange').

The use of the word to define a regular arrangement has been a feature of English since about 1200.

b) The ecclesiastical use of the word to denote specific monastic societies dates from the twelfth century when the religious life attracted those who for one reason or another wished to cut themselves off from the rest of the populace and join a 'line' of monks. The practice has also spawned expressions such as 'to take Holy Orders' (i.e., study theology) and 'to be ordained' (i.e., become a minister of the church).

c) 'To give orders' in either a civilian or military context has its origins in the latter. Soldiers have subjected themselves to being 'ordered' to perform certain tasks since the 1540s, although originally an 'order' would have been an instruction issued to soldiers to form into clearly defined or 'ordered' ranks.

d) The commercial use of 'ordering' a book, suit, etc., dates from the nineteenth century and is really another way of telling somebody to do something. When customers order an item in a shop, they are simply instructing the owner to obtain it for them. This is an echo of the Old English verb *besprecan* ('to speak about' or 'to complain'). In Middle English the notion of complaining had been lost and the reformed verb *bespeken* meant 'to talk about' or 'to discuss'. Such conversations would have frequently led to a customer placing an 'order' with a tradesman, artisan, etc., until eventually advanced orders were referred to as 'bespoken'. The term survives in the modern English expression 'bespoke tailor'.

PACE

Examples: a) He set off at a cracking **pace** and disappeared from sight.

b) Their parents took them **pace** egging in the park.

a) The word 'pace' has been used to denote speed or acceleration since the early sixteenth century and is derived from the Latin *passus*, the passive past participle of the verb *pandere* ('to stretch'). For the Romans, then, the basic idea of what was involved in going for a good walk was not all that far removed from the modern English expression 'to stretch one's legs'. The same word was used as a Roman unit of measurement in the term *mille passus* ('a thousand steps') which turns up in English as a 'mile'.

The French also borrowed the Latin expression as *pas* for 'a step' but bestowed upon it the additional meaning of a 'mountain defile'. After some time the French word entered English, but the 'steps' were now forgotten and only the association with gaps between the mountains retained, hence our mountain 'passes'.

The Latin verb *pandere* has, of course, also provided the modern English 'to expand', which is basically a synonym of 'to stretch'.

b) Of absolutely no connection whatever with Roman soldiers is the expression 'pace egging'. In many parts of Britain this custom has now largely died out, but it is still preserved in parts of the north, particularly Lancashire. Every Easter the crowds gather in local parks and roll their highly decorated eggs (though it must be admitted that nowadays most of these are made of chocolate) known as 'pace' eggs. The derivation here is the Hebrew word *pesakh* ('Passover') but it is probably more recognizable in other languages' words for Easter: *Pâcques* (French), *Pascua* (Spanish), and *Pasqua* (Italian).

The expression 'pace eggs' dates from approximately 1610, and 'Easter eggs' are thought to be an invention of the 1820s.

PAGE

Examples: a) He did not want to be dressed as a **page** boy at the wedding.

b) She tore out the **page** with the recipe on it.

a) When the Normans invaded England and began to alter the language that had been the common means of communication for centuries, the masculine noun *page* was one of the words they brought with them. The basic meaning of the word was 'young servant', and it had been absorbed into Norman French from the Italian *paggio* with more or less the same meaning. *Paggio* too had made its way into Italian from Greek, in which the normal word for a small boy or child was *paidion*. The same word, in a somewhat altered form, has provided us with the prefix 'paedo-' which appears in many words and expressions used in modern English. We now have 'paedophilia', in which 'paedo-' combines with the Greek verb *philein* 'I love' and so means 'love of children'. Then there is the same prefix combined with the Greek for 'doctor', *iatros*, which produces 'paediatrician', a doctor who specializes in the medical problems of young children.

b) Another French word the Normans gave us was the grammatically feminine *page*. This time the word of course means 'page' in the sense of a leaf from a book. The basic Indo-European root here is **pak* ('to bind') and its association with the modern meaning is fairly clear. Originally the Latin word *pagina* (from which the French term was descended) was a reference to the practice of binding strips of papyrus together in a continuous strip or scroll. Then, when somebody had the idea of binding the strips together at the sides instead of at the top and bottom, the book (a collection of pages) was born.

Surprisingly, however, this invention of the 'page' is associated linguistically with another apparently totally unrelated concept, 'peace'. The Indo-European **pak* is also the origin of the Latin *pax* ('peace'), and this derivation provides us with an insight into how the ancients thought. If we are not at war with our neighbours, we are 'bound' to them, possibly in order to wage war against a common enemy. A similarly derivative word is 'pact'. If we enter into a 'pact' with our neighbours, there is a 'bond' between us, allowing us to coexist in an atmosphere of 'peace' and harmony.

PAN

Examples: a) 'Boil some eggs in the little **pan**,' she said to her husband.
   b) The teacher told his pupils about the Greek god called **Pan**.
   c) **Pan** American Airways was usually known as **Pan** Am.
   d) The photographer wanted to **pan** the whole room.

a) The English word 'pan' has come down to us from the Latin *patina* ('a dish'), which in turn can trace its origin back to the Greek *patanē* with the same meaning. Another associated Latin word was *patella*, also a dish but this time one specifically designed and used for making offerings to the gods. In the modern world *patella* has retained its culinary associations and re-emerged in the Spanish dish known universally as 'paella'.

Patella, of course, is now used in English as the medical term for the dish-shaped bone more generally referred to as the 'kneecap'. And *patina* now defines the age-related protective sheen furniture acquires as it matures. It might seem a long way from a Roman housewife's kitchen utensil to a modern term for the condition of an antique table but the link is clear if we remember that a dish can also serve as a protective covering.

b) We don't have to be classics scholars to know about Pan, the Greek god usually depicted as having the legs and horns of a goat and a predilection for playing pipes. The name basically means 'feeder' and is derived from an Indo-European **pa-* ('to feed'); the same root that has given us the words 'pastor' (one who makes sure his flock is fed) and 'pasture' (a feeding ground). It also produced the words for bread in various European languages: French has *pain*, Spanish has *pan*, and Italian has *pane*. Another allied word in English is 'pantry', which was formerly a place where only bread was kept. Rather surprisingly, a further associated word is 'panic', which was originally the fear experienced when being pursued through the woods by the god Pan.

c) 'Pan-' is frequently used in English as a prefix to mean 'all' or 'universal'. This use has come directly from ancient Greek for 'all': *pas* (masculine), *pasa* (feminine), and *pan* (neuter). We now see it used in expressions such as pan-American, pan-European, pan-Hellenic, etc., It also turns up in words such as 'panacea' (a cure-all), 'pancreas' (all flesh), and 'pandemic' (an illness affecting all the people). And if we describe a disorderly, noisy gathering as 'pandemo-nium', this time we are using the word to say that the scene we are witnessing looks as if 'all the demons' have been set loose.

d) To talk of 'panning' with a camera is to use an abbreviated form of 'panorama', a noun taken from the Greek *pan* ('everything') and *horaein* ('to see') and meaning 'everything seen'.

PAWN

Examples: a) He moved the **pawn** and took his opponent's rook.
           b) She redeemed her ring from the **pawn** shop.

a) The word had been known in French as *poun* since the thirteenth century, and when it was adopted into English in the fourteenth it retained the same spelling; the spelling we recognize today was a later development. It is the least powerful piece on the chessboard and its lowly position is reflected in the derivation of the word. French acquired the word from the Spanish *peón*, meaning a 'foot soldier' which in turn was derived from the Latin *pes* ('foot'). *Peón* survives in modern Spanish both as a chess piece and as a term denoting an 'unskilled workman'.

A commonly used cognate noun in English is 'pioneer'. We now think of a pioneer as somebody who leads the way in almost any field of human activity (the first use of the word with this meaning dates from around 1600), but originally he would have been one of a band of foot soldiers who cleared the way or prepared roads ahead of an army's advance.

The figurative use of the word 'pawn' denoting people cynically manipulated by those in positions of authority dates from around the 1580s.

b) The 'pawnbroker' is linguistically someone who deals in 'pawns' or 'pledges'. The word itself is derived from Old French *pan*, supposedly a borrowing from the prehistoric Germanic root **panda* and a relative of the modern German *Pfand* ('pledge' or 'security on a loan'). Ultimately, however, the word may be derived from the Latin *pignus* ('pledge') and the verb *pignerare* ('to give as a pledge', 'to pawn', or 'to mortgage').

There is another interesting linguistic association here. The first pawnbrokers' shops in England were established by the Italian Lombard family in the thirteenth century, and an early term for the rooms on which the pledges, or 'pawns', were stored were known as 'Lombard rooms' (an early term for a pawnbroker was a 'Lombardeer'). Over time this evolved into 'lumber rooms' and later still, around the sixteenth or seventeenth century, the word 'lumber' acquired its modern meaning of 'superfluous, unwanted rubbish'.

PEN

Examples: a) She wrote to her aunt with her brand new fountain **pen**.
b) The sheep were driven into a **pen** for the night.
c) A female swan is known as a **pen**.
d) He spent several years in the state **pen**.

a) The link may appear tenuous, but this use of the word 'pen' has its origins in the Indo-European root **pet* ('to fly'). The linguistic association becomes clearer when we consider that the Old French *penne* and Latin *penna*, the origins of the English word, were terms for 'feather', used as an early writing implement. It also explains why we refer to small folding pocket knives as 'penknives'. They were originally designed for sharpening the tips of feathers to make writing on parchment easier and the finished product more legible. The other term for this kind of writing tool was a 'quill', which has given linguists a bit of a headache as it lacks a definitive etymological explanation. It is, however, just possible that the word is derived from the Middle High German *kil* meaning 'goose feather'.

It is interesting to note that the French for a pen is *plume*, a word cognate with English 'plumage'.

b) Old English had a word, *penn*, used to define a small enclosure. There is a certain amount of doubt about the origin of the usage also, but some etymologists are of the opinion that it is ultimately from the Latin *pinna* (an alternative form of *penna*), which, in addition to 'feather', possibly referred to any sharpened or tapering stick, such as those we would now refer to as 'pins'. The implication here is that in Anglo-Saxon times, when sheep had been ushered into an enclosure, the gate would have been shut and secured by some sort of locking device involving perhaps a crude hasp, staple, and pin.

c) Since the sixteenth century female swans have been referred to as 'pens' (the males are known as 'cobs') but nobody really knows why. Some linguists have tried to associate the word with the Celtic word *penn* ('head'), but the etymological connection is still a matter of debate.

d) The use of the word to designate a prison is an Americanism. It is an abbreviation for 'penitentiary', a word derived from the Latin *poena*, generally meaning a punishment but originally the money paid as a fine for having committed a crime. This was a direct borrowing from the Greek *poinē*, a fine paid for the shedding of blood. And the Romans and Greeks personified punishment as Poena and Poinē respectively, the goddesses of vengeance.

PERCH

Examples: a) The **perch** is to be found in many European rivers.

b) An owl was sitting patiently on its **perch**.

a) It might seem a convoluted linguistic journey but the fish known as the 'perch' takes its name from the colour of grapes maturing on the vine in ancient Greece. It entered English around 1300 as a borrowing from the French *perche*, from the Latin *perca*, itself taken from the Greek *perkē*. The Greek noun, however, was directly linked to the adjective *perknos* meaning 'spotted' or 'variegated' on account of the shading and colouring on the fish's skin. But *perknos* was originally a description not of fish but of the increasingly dark colour of grapes as they ripen on the vine; the Greeks even had a specific verb for this process, *perkazein* ('to turn dark'). The Indo-European root of all these associated words was **perk* ('speckled' or 'spotted').

b) In the thirteenth century a 'perch' referred to almost any pole, stick, or rod. But in the fourteenth century it acquired a more specific meaning as a unit of linear measurement: 5.5 yards (or five metres). Also in the fourteenth century, the word was used to denote a horizontal length of wood on which hawks and other tame birds could land or 'perch'. A century later it was being used with the more general meaning of a 'resting place' for birds of any description.

The Old French term (from which the English is borrowed) was *perche* and this had in turn found its way into the language from the Latin *pertica* ('a long pole', particularly one which could have been used as a measuring rod). And the Latin form, it is believed, was directly related to the Umbrian word *perkaf*, meaning simply a bundle of sticks or twigs.

There is an interesting cognate in modern usage. The English word 'perk' is a variant of 'perch' and if we exhort somebody to 'perk up', what we are advising them to do is to sit up straight and behave the way a bird on a perch behaves when it is preening itself.

PILE

Examples: a) There was a **pile** of clothes by the washing machine.

b) The engineers drove **piles** into the sea bed.

c) She bought a thick-**pile** carpet for the living room.

d) Peter went to the doctor to see about his **piles**.

a) Anything gathered up into a heap has been referred to as a 'pile' in English since the fifteenth century. The basic idea is the same as that behind the word 'pillar', to which it is closed allied linguistically. And 'pillar' is from the Latin *pila*, which meant the same as modern English 'pillar' but was also the Roman term for a 'pier' or 'mole'. In this sense, a *pila* comprised 'piles' of stones gathered together and arranged on the beach to provide some protection to a harbour from the elements. The associated verb here was *pangere* ('to secure', 'to fix', or 'to drive in').

b) A 'pile' meaning a pointed stake driven into the ground as part of a wooden wall or fence has existed in English since the eleventh century, although the word was used in Old English (as *pīl*) to refer to a sharpened stick or arrow. The Latin word from which it is derived was *pilum*, and this had two distinct meanings: it could define either (i) a heavy throwing spear or javelin used by Roman foot soldiers or (ii) the kitchen appliance known as a 'pestle'. The common denominator here is probably the heavy weight, as *pilum* was derived from the verb *pinso* ('to stamp on' or 'to crush').

c) The nap on cloth has been referred to as the 'pile' since the 1560s and can trace its origin back to the Latin for a single hair, *pilus*. This is related to another Latin noun, *pileus* (alternatively *pilleum*) the term for a close-fitting felt cap worn on feast days and by slaves after they had been freed from bondage. Its cognate noun in Greek was *pilos* which probably holds the key to how a word for a single hair is connected with a felt cap. *Pilos* referred specifically to felt that had been wrought from individual strands of hair or wool.

d) The medical condition known colloquially as 'piles' is cognate with the word 'pellet', a diminutive of the Latin *pila* ('ball'; unconnected with *pila* ('pillar')) therefore meaning 'a little ball'. The scientific name for 'piles' is 'haemorrhoids', from the Greek *haima* ('blood') and *rhein* ('to flow'), as the condition is character-ized by persistent bleeding.

POACH

Examples: a) When the toast was ready she began to **poach** the eggs.
          b) He was fined £150 and told not to **poach** on the estate again.

a) The idea behind poaching eggs (as opposed to frying or boiling them) is to cook them in such a way that when served the white seems to form a 'pouch' (borrowed from the French *poche* ('bag')) around the yolk. The use of the word in this context dates from the fifteenth century.

The Middle English version of the word was *poke*, which we still use today in the expression 'to buy a pig in a poke'. The warning implicit in the expression is that we should never buy anything without examining it first, as would be the case if we bought a pig in an unopened bag or pouch.

And of course the word *poke* is the origin of what we refer to today as a 'pocket'.

b) There are two theories as to how catching fish or game illegally came to be known as 'poaching'. There are those who believe that the word is associated with pockets or pouches; i.e., a poacher would catch his prey, kill it, and then take it home in his pocket or bag.

The other theory is that it is derived from the Old French word *poucier* or *pochier* ('thumb') and its related verb *peucher* ('to prod or pierce with the thumb'). If this is the case, it is the idea of intrusion that is behind our modern expression. A man who goes out at night to do a bit of poaching inevitably has to force his way (or at least enter by stealth) onto property which he knows should be out of bounds.

Other associated words here are 'to poke', which originally meant to prod with one's thumb, and 'poker', an instrument seen on every hearth in every house in the land when the only source of heat was a coal fire. And fires needed to be 'poked' every now and then to rearrange the coals and shake out the ash and cinders.

POLE

Examples: a) He knocked a **pole** into the ground as a boundary marker.
b) The **Poles** and Czechs took part in the Battle of Britain.
c) The weather is very cold at the North **Pole**.

a) In ancient Rome a *palus* could refer to any kind of a pole or stake, but in a military context it also had a very definite meaning. All recruits to the army went through a rigorous period of training, a large part of which was dedicated to developing combat skills and the *palus* would have been much in evidence on any training ground. It was a section of a tree fixed (the derivative verb is *pangere* ('to secure')) in the ground and against which the trainee soldiers learned how to slash and stab with a sword. Eventually the word was adopted into many European languages, usually without the martial implications. Old English had *pal*, Old High German *pfal*, Old Norse *pall*, and Dutch has *paal*. The spelling and pronunciation changed from 'pal' to 'pole' in English some time after the thirteenth century.

b) Poland and its inhabitants take their name from the fact that vast areas of the land in that part of the world are very flat. The Indo-European root **pele* meant 'flat' or 'spread out' and produced a myriad of terms in several European languages. *Polje* in Russian and *pole* in Polish mean 'field', and historically the Poles referred to themselves as *polanie* ('those who live in the fields'). Also allied linguistically is the Greek *platus* ('wide', 'flat', or 'broad'), which has spawned words such as 'place' in English (and also 'plaice', a variety of 'flatfish'), *place* in French, *piazza* in Italian, *plaza* in Spanish, and *Platz* in German. It also gave one of the most important philosophers of all time his nickname: Plato. He was really Aristoklēs (died c. 347 BC), but was known as *platōn* ('the broad one') some say because he had broad shoulders, others because he had a broad forehead, and yet others because of the breadth of his knowledge

c) The history of this use of the word suggests that in ancient times the top and bottom of the world were thought to be where the axis around which the earth spun had its exit points. The word was used in English with this meaning from the late fourteenth century, derived as it was from the Latin *polus* ('the end of an axis') and the Greek *polos* ('a pivot'). The derivative verb here is *pelesthai* ('to be in motion').

POLICY

Examples: a) He took out a life insurance **policy** when he got married.
b) It was a matter of company **policy** to pay the workers well.

a) The word 'policy' has existed in English as proof of an agreement between a client and an insurance company since around the 1560s. It was a borrowing from French *police* ('contract') which the French had borrowed from the Italian *polizza* as a term for written proof that a commercial transaction had been entered into.

The medieval Latin word from which both the Italian and French terms were derived was *apodissa*, a receipt for monies paid, which in turn had been acquired from the ancient Greek *deiknunai* ('to show'; from the Indo-European root **deik* ('show')) with its compound related verb *apodeiknunai* ('to prove that something is').

b) When used to define a course of action, the word 'policy' has no connection whatever with documentary proof but is yet another word derived from the Greek. In ancient Greece an independent city state (such as Athens or Sparta) was a *polis*, a term derived from the Indo-European root **pele* ('citadel' or 'enclosed space') and the Sanskrit *puram* ('town'). The manner in which a *polis* or town was administered or governed was known in Greek as *politeia*, the source of the modern English 'policy'. In the modern world, the body of citizens tasked with ensuring that the *politeia* of the land is observed is generally known as the 'police' force.

A closely connected expression was *politikē tekhnē* ('the art or science of citizenship' or, as we would now call it, 'politics'). The ancient Greeks considered it quite normal for a citizen to want to take part in *politikē tekhnē*, but it was also accepted that there were some people who preferred to keep to themselves. Such people were known as *idiōtes* (from *idios* ('personal' or 'private')), a term which has given us the modern English word 'idiot'.

PORT

Examples: a) The boat sank as it was leaving **port**.

b) **Port** and starboard are naval terms for left and right.

c) Colonel Smithers always enjoyed a glass of **port** after dinner.

a) All these usages share a common ancestor and can be traced back to the Greek word *peran* which essentially meant 'I pass through' and its associated noun *porthmos* ('ferry', 'strait', or 'crossing by ferry'). However, the verb *peran* had a secondary meaning of 'I carry goods beyond the seas for sale' and the goods so delivered were, more often than not, slaves. By the time the word was adopted into Latin it had produced two further nouns *porta* and *portus*, the former referring to city gates (and subsequently to any gate or door), the latter being used for a harbour or 'port'.

There is a fascinating linguistic link here: the adjective 'opportune' is derived from the Latin expression *ob portum veniens* ('coming towards port'). Any wind blowing in such a direction would have made it easier for ships to enter the harbour and would thus be considered favourable or, as we might say, 'opportune'. And this, of course, is also the origin of the noun 'opportunity'.

b) The two sides of a boat were originally referred to as the 'larboard' and 'starboard'. Larboard was the side on which goods were loaded (Middle English *laddeborde*), and the other side was where the paddle or other steering mechanism was housed. The term for this in Old English was *stēorbord*, which eventually evolved into 'starboard'.

In 1844 the Royal Navy decided to dispense with the term 'larboard' as it was so easily confused with 'starboard', particularly in a high wind when sailors would have had the greatest difficulty distinguishing between the two. The alternative term selected was 'port'.

c) The fortified wine, port, takes its name from its place of origin, Oporto (from *o porto*, Portuguese for 'the port') on the western coast of Portugal. And in fact, the country itself was known to the Romans as Portus Cale, a combination of the Latin *portus* and *Cale*, thought to be a Celtic place name. Some linguists suggest a possible connection with the Greek *kalos* ('beautiful').

POST

Examples: a) He hung his hat on a **post** fixed in the ground.
b) She worked in a **post** office all her life.
c) The police asked for a **post**-mortem on the body.

a) The consensus among etymologists is that the derivation of this kind of 'post' is somewhat unclear and that the most likely linguistic association is with the Latin *postis* ('doorpost'). It has further been suggested that this word is itself derived from the preposition *pro* ('in front of') and the verb *stare* ('to stand'), suggesting that the original Latin 'post' simply 'stood in front' of the house. On the other hand, there is also the suggestion that the word is a straightforward development of *positus*, the passive past participle of *ponere* ('to put'), and thus is basically nothing more than a length of timber that has been 'put' into the ground.

b) The association with letters, packages, etc., that have to be delivered from one part of the country to another is essentially military in nature. As the Roman Empire expanded and it was deemed necessary to protect all lines of communication, soldiers would have been stationed at various places along the roads to protect travellers and traders on their journeys. Such protection units would have been 'posted' at regular intervals and expected to remain at their 'posts' until ordered to leave. Over the centuries these places developed into 'staging posts' where travellers (civilian as well as military) could have a meal, rest, and change horses before continuing on their way. It was presumably not long before somebody had the idea of asking such wayfarers travelling between 'posts' to deliver important letters or documents to residents in other parts of the country, and thus the first 'postal' service came into being.

c) In modern English it is quite common, if not the norm, to talk about a 'post-mortem' as if it were a noun. This is, strictly speaking, incorrect since *post mortem* in Latin means 'after death' and is used as an adjectival phrase; the full expression should be 'a post-mortem examination'.

The Latin *post* ('after') has been adopted into many English expressions and is used frequently in everyday language: to 'post-date' a cheque'; a 'postgraduate' student; a 'postdoctoral' thesis; an award can be granted 'posthumously' (literally 'after the recipient has been buried in the ground'); and, of course, if we write a letter and then think of something to say after the main body of the writing is finished, we add a PS, the conventional abbreviation for *postscriptum*, the Latin for 'written after'.

POUND

Examples: a) She paid a **pound** for a **pound** of beans.

b) The stray dogs were taken to the **pound**.

c) She began to **pound** the mixture to a soft paste.

a) A 'pound' as a unit of weight and a 'pound' as a unit of currency share a common linguistic origin. Its association with weight is derived from the Latin *pondo*, meaning 'by weight' from the noun **pondus* ('weight') which occurs only rarely in the nominative. The verb associated with these words is *pendere* ('to weigh' or 'to hang'), which produced a more figurative verb *ponderare* ('to weigh up'), the origin of the modern English verb 'to ponder'.

Our word 'pound' is further connected with the Latin expression *libra pondo* ('a pound by weight') where *libra* originally meant the scales in which money, grain, etc., would have been 'weighed out'. And *libra* is the origin of our abbreviation for the pound as a unit of weight, 'lb'.

The Latin verb *pendere* has also given us words such as 'pension' (an amount of money 'weighed' or 'assessed' as adequate for a person's needs) and 'pendant' (an article of adornment 'hanging down' from somebody's neck).

b) As an enclosure (originally for cattle), 'pound' is thought to be related to the word 'pond', which is a similar kind of enclosure, albeit one in which water is contained by the surrounding land. The Old English term was *pund*, and this in turn was connected to *punfald*, a tautological term combining 'pen' and 'fold', both of which can refer to small enclosures where animals can be kept. A closely related English term is 'pinfold', derived from the Old English verb *pyndan* ('to shut up' or 'to confine').

c) In the word 'pound' meaning to beat, the final 'd' is a later addition, as the original Old English word was *punian* and the Middle English *pounen*, both of which meant 'to bruise' in a mortar. Interestingly, at least one authoritative etymologist (Walter Skeat) suggests that the same word is the origin of the word 'pun' (a play on words). The reasoning here is that a pun is an attempt to 'beat' additional meanings out of a word or expression.

PUNCH

Examples: a) He could **punch** like a man half his age.

b) A couple of glasses of **punch** and she was all tipsy.

c) Every seaside town used to have a **Punch** and Judy show.

a) There are two meanings of the verb 'to punch' as it is used in modern English, although ultimately they share the same origin. The use of the word to mean 'striking somebody with a clenched fist' dates from around the 1570s and is related to the Latin *pugnare*, which is also the origin of the English adjective 'pugnacious'. Prior to this date 'to punch' was more associated with piercing, prodding, etc., with a pointed tool known as a 'puncheon'. This appeared in the mid-fourteenth century as a borrowing from the French *ponchon*, derived from the Latin *pungere* ('to prick' or 'to stab'). Other common English words related to this are 'puncture' (to make a hole in) and 'punctuate' (to make marks in a manuscript which resembled little holes).

b) 'Punch' as an alcoholic beverage was introduced to England in the seventeenth century by travellers and tradesmen returning from exotic lands such as India. The word is supposedly derived from the Hindi *panch* ('five') as the drink contained five ingredients: sugar, water, lemon juice, alcohol, and spice. And the Hindi *panch* combined with the Persian *ab* ('water') in the name of the area known in its anglicized form as the 'Punjab', literally the land of the 'five waters' or rivers: the Beas, Chenab, Jhelum, Ravi, and Sutlej.

c) Mr Punch and his wife, Judy (who, incidentally, was originally Joan), are products of the sixteenth-century form of Italian entertainment known as *commedia dell'arte*. The seventeenth-century diarist Samuel Pepys describes what is probably one of the couple's first appearances in England, in London's Covent Garden in 1662. The name 'Punch' is a shortened form of Punchinello, the anglicized version of the Italian *Pulcinella*, thought to be a corrupted form of *pollecena*, 'young turkey'. This is a possible reference to the puppet's nose, likened by many to a bird's beak.

The descriptive phrase 'as pleased as Punch' is usually interpreted as a reference to Mr Punch's unfailing ability to get the better of anyone who opposes him.

PUPIL

Examples: a) Jane was considered the most gifted **pupil** in the school.

b) The **pupil** of one eye was dilated.

a) The association between a classroom and a 'pupil' did not occur until the middle of the sixteenth century. Prior to that, 'pupil' was a term applied to orphans or children who for one reason or another were being brought up by a ward or guardian. The word came into English from the Old French *pupille*, which in turn was a derivative of the Latin *pupillus* ('an orphan boy') and *pupilla* ('an orphan girl'). Both of these nouns were derived from the normal terms of endearment for boy and girl, *pupus* and *pupa*, as simple alternatives to the standard words *puer* and *puella*. The Indo-European root from which the Latin terms are derived is *pu/*pup/*peu* ('to swell', 'to inflate', and 'to beget').

Modern cognates include: 'pupa', an insect at the stage of development when it is also referred to as a chrysalis; 'puppet', from the French *poupette* and the Vulgar Latin *puppa* ('doll'); and the word 'puppy'. The Old English for a young dog was *hwelp* (modern English 'whelp') and the term 'puppy' at the time it entered into English in the fifteenth century referred to what we now think of as a 'lapdog'.

b) It was also in the fifteenth century that the idea of a little boy or girl was adopted to define part of the eye. And once again, it would seem the custom crept into English from Latin via Old French. The Romans noticed that if we stand close enough to another person to see a reflection in their eyes, what we see is a diminutive form of ourselves. In other words, the image we see resembles a *pupilla*, or little doll.

QUACK

Examples: a) All ducks **quack**.

b) A colloquial term for a doctor is **quack**.

a) The obvious explanation for the sound made by a duck is that it is simply imitative, but there is a surprise when we examine the etymology of the word. In the fourteenth century the word was *quelke*, and it was not until the sixteenth century that 'quake' entered the language and then evolved into the form we recognize today. The immediate ancestor of both variants is the Latin *coaxere* 'to croak'. Earlier, however, the Greeks had the noun *koax*, a comic attempt at emulating not the sound made by ducks but the croaking noise produced by frogs.

b) The unflattering term 'quack', as applied to a doctor, dates back to the time when no training or medical qualifications were needed before a 'doctor' could treat the sick and sell them his unproven medicines. The derivation of the term is Old Dutch *quacksalver* (literally a hawker of salve or healing potions and ointments; modern Dutch *kwakzalver*).

The first element of the word is derived from the Middle Dutch verb *quacken* ('to boast'), and the second is cognate with the Old English *sealf* ('healing oil' or 'ointment'). Hence the original *quacksalver* was a tradesman who walked the streets of medieval towns and villages boasting about how good his healing oils were.

'Salve' is related to the late Latin *salvare* ('to save' or 'to make secure'), which is thought to be related to the Sanskrit *sarpis* ('melted butter'). Possibly the ancients had a somewhat exaggerated idea of the healing properties of the greasy substance, but as the Indo-European root here is *selp* ('fat') the link would appear to be not all that far-fetched.

QUARREL

Examples: a) He does not **quarrel** with his wife very often.

b) The **quarrel** struck the knight in the left shoulder.

a) In Old French the noun *querele* meant 'business', 'concern', or 'dispute'. Presumably the reason for the close association between argument and business dealings is the recognition that when people are discussing financial or commercial matters, there is always a good chance that sooner or later serious disagreement will occur. Modern French has retained the idea of disagreement with *querelle* and also a curious associated expression: *une querelle d'Allemand*. This literally means 'a German quarrel' and is used by the French to describe 'an argument over nothing'. Modern French also has the expression is *chercher noise* ('to pick a quarrel with'), from the Old French word *noise* ('loud clamour'), the source of modern English 'noise'. Both are ultimately derived from the Latin *nausea* ('sea sickness', 'annoyance', or 'disgust').

The modern English, modern French, and Old French all derive their words from the Latin *querella* ('complaint' or 'accusation'), and the verb *queri* ('to complain' or 'to lament').

b) The crossbow made its appearance on the battlefields of Europe in medieval times. It brought great changes to the tactics of warfare as the new weapon was capable of inflicting terrible injuries on opposing forces; armoured knights in particular were made redundant by the bolts or 'quarrels' which could punch a hole in all but the thickest armour.

The 'quarrel' in this context has no linguistic connection with the synonym for a heated argument. It takes its name from the Old French *quarel* or *carrel*, derived from the Late Latin adjective *quadrus* meaning 'square'. The reference here is to the 'square' cross section of the bolt, as opposed to the more traditional arrows which had a circular cross section.

QUARRY

Examples: a) The hounds got a strong whiff of their **quarry**.
          b) His father works in a **quarry** in North Wales.

a) In the fourteenth century the Middle English word *querre* or *quirre* was used to describe the dismembered parts of a deer which had been wrapped in an animal skin and presented to the hounds as a reward for a successful kill. In the fifteenth century the term was applied to animals caught and killed by hawks, and then by 1610 it was used more generally to refer to any creature chased in a hunt.

There are several accounts as to the derivation of the word, but linguists seem to agree that the most likely origin is the Middle French *curée* ('entrails'). This in turn is derived from the Vulgar Latin **corata* ('viscera' or 'entrails'), from the Latin word for *cor* ('heart'). The alternative suggestions are that the word can be traced back either to the Latin *corium* ('skin' or 'hide') or to the confusion between two French words: *cuir* ('skin') and *curer* ('to cleanse by removing the entrails').

b) In the fifteenth century the word *quarrere* was used to denote a place where rock was fashioned into stones with regular square-shaped sides which builders could use to construct humble houses and magnificent cathedrals alike. The Old

French term for such a place was *quarriere*, from the late Latin *quadrarie*, acquired from the Latin noun *quadrum* ('a square').

But another Latin word provides a further clue to the evolution of the word. A *quadratarius* in ancient Rome was a particularly skilled mason whose job it was to give a 'square' shape to amorphous rocks. Over time, however, the term was applied less to specialist craftsmen and increasingly to stonecutters in general. And the places where these workers chiselled rough stone into recognizable shapes came to be associated less with skilled labour and more with the basic process of extracting the rock from the ground. This, of course, is how we understand the word 'quarry' today.

RAPE

Examples: a) In most countries **rape** is considered a very serious crime.
b) **Rape** is a valuable crop in some parts of the world.
c) A **rape** is an old land measure in southern England.

a) 'Rape' as a criminal offence is now almost always associated with sexual violence, but a brief look at the history of the word shows that this was not always the case. In fact, the word only acquired its present meaning around the sixteenth century; previously, it signified theft by force, particularly if committed with speed. A good clue to this interpretation is the fact that 'rape' is cognate with the adjective 'rapid', and both words are derived from the Latin *rapere* ('to grab') and the Indo-European root **rep* ('to snatch'). Another surprising link is with the noun 'rapture', which since the early seventeenth century has had the sense of 'captured by' or 'carried away by' in a spiritual or emotional, rather than physical, sense.

b) The beautiful yellow crop known as 'rape' (or rapeseed), which is such an economically important commodity in many countries of the world, has nothing to do with snatching or sexual aggression. It is linked etymologically with the Latin *rapum* ('turnip'), which in turn is distantly (and somewhat puzzlingly) with three Greek vegetables: the *rhaphē* was the ancient Greek term for a 'large radish'; a *rhaphanis* was a 'small radish'; and a *rhaphanos* was a 'cabbage'. In the modern world a turnip in Russian is a *repa*, and the Italian dish known as *ravioli* is an additional cognate.

'Rape' is also used in the winemaking industry as the term for the pulp left over after the juice has been squeezed out of the grape. But there appears to be no linguistic connection between the words 'rape' and 'grape', and the derivation of this usage of the word is unclear.

c) Mainly of interest to historians, a 'rape' in the southern English county of Sussex was a specified unit of land. Until the nineteenth century the county was divided into six 'rapes', and the usual explanation of the term is that it is linked linguistically with the Old English *rape*, meaning 'rope'. The common assumption is that the areas so designated were cordoned off from each other by ropes (or perhaps rope fences) for legal and administrative purposes.

RENT

Examples: a) Times were hard and they could not pay the **rent**.

b) The knife made a **rent** three inches long in the cloth.

a) This is a word firmly fixed in the feudal history of England. By the thirteenth century 'rent' (from the Old French *rente*) was being used to mean payment made in exchange for the use of land or property by a tenant, and the related verb *renter* meant 'to pay what is due'. This was a variant of another Old French verb *render* ('to give back' or 'to yield'), a verb closely allied to the Vulgar Latin *rendere* and its feminine passive past participle *rendita* ('that which has been rendered or returned'). The Modern English 'rent' is an abbreviated form of *moneta rendita* meaning 'money rendered'.

At some point in the thirteenth century another Old French expression was adopted into English. The feminine noun *ferme* was now being used for 'rent', from the medieval Latin *firma* ('fixed payment') and the Latin *firmus* ('firm' or 'fixed'). It was not until the sixteenth century that the derivative word 'farm' was used in English to denote land or property, as opposed to the money paid in exchange for its use. Consequently, in the fourteenth century the original 'farmers' were bailiffs or rent collectors, and the term was not applied until the sixteenth century to the people who tilled the land.

b) 'To rend' meaning 'to tear' has existed in English in its present form since the 1530s. Prior to that, it had existed in Middle English from the early fourteenth century as *renten*, a variant of the Old English *rendan* or *hrendan* ('to tear down'). The derivation of these forms was the West Germanic **randijan*, cognate with the modern German *Rinde* ('bark', 'crust', or 'rind'). Its etymology would therefore suggest that the original meaning of the word was 'to tear something off', rather than simply to make a hole in it.

ROCKET

Examples: a) The **rocket** shot into the sky and exploded.

b) **Rocket** in salad is not everybody's favourite.

a) Virtually all rockets, whether they are used for military purposes, to explore space, or simply to add exciting aerial pyrotechnics to a firework display have one thing in common: their shape. They are always cylindrical and resemble narrow and sometimes enormously long tubes. This is a clue to the etymology of the word. There are several European languages that seem to have contributed to the form of the word which eventually made its way into English. Middle High German had *rocke*, Middle Dutch had *rocke*, and Italian had *rocca*, which all meant 'distaff' (the cylindrical bobbin used by the spinsters of yesteryear as they sat at their spinning wheels turning wool into thread). The diminutive form in Italian, *roccheto*, is now taken to be the immediate antecedent of the word 'rocket' as it appears in English. The term 'rocket' defining a self-propelled missile dates from the early seventeenth century.

The promise or threat 'to give somebody a rocketing' because their behaviour has warranted a stern reprimand is a borrowing from the early use of rockets as a weapon of war. To be subjected to rocket attack on the battle field was (and still is) considered a very unpleasant experience, and so anybody subjected to a metaphorical 'rocketing' would feel similarly uncomfortable.

b) The slightly peppery, leafy vegetable that can make a pleasant addition to a salad takes its name from the Latin *eruca* ('colewort'; i.e. a cabbage which has its top cut off before it becomes firm). In Roman times a young cabbage was referred to as an *eruca* because its stem was covered with spiky hairs that resembled the spines on the *ericius* ('hedgehog'). A further connection is the verb *erigere* ('to erect' or 'to become upright'; i.e., in the manner of a hedgehog's spines).

ROOM

Examples: a) The dogs had plenty of **room** to run about in the garden.
b) She had a very small **room** in which to study.

a) In Old English and Middle English the word *rum* did not refer to individual apartments or sections within a house. *Rum* was used in the much wider sense of 'space' and even had the extended meaning of 'scope' or 'opportunity'. Cognate with the modern German *Raum*, the word is derived from the Indo-European root **reue* ('to open'), which also gave us words such as 'rustic' and 'rural' via the Latin *rus* ('countryside'). This is also the root of the Latin *rusticari* ('to live in the country' and later 'to banish to the countryside'). In the seventeenth century this gave rise to the English verb 'to rusticate' meaning 'to retire to the country' in order to escape the hustle and bustle of city life. Universities later 'rusticated' (or temporarily sent down) students for poor academic performance or misdemeanours.

b) Until the mid-fifteenth century an individual part or section of a house was referred to as a 'chamber', and it was only after this date that the term was replaced by 'room'.

In Old English the term for what we would now call a 'room' was *cofa*, from the Old Norse *kofi* ('shed' or 'hut'). This, of course, is the modern word 'cove', which we now think of as referring to a small sheltered inlet or bay on the coast.

It is tempting to find an etymological link between *cove, kofi*, and 'alcove'; but there is none. The word 'alcove' (a small recess in a room) entered English as a borrowing from Spanish *alcoba* ('bedroom'). This in turn is a borrowing from Arabic *al-qubba* ('the vault').

'Cove' as a synonym for 'man' is totally unrelated. It is a direct borrowing from the Romany word *cova* ('man').

SACK

Examples: a) He put the gun in an old **sack** and threw it in the lake.
                b) They feared the enemy would **sack** the town.
                c) Shakespeare's character Falstaff liked a glass of **sack**.
                d) She was given the **sack** after just one day in the job.

a) Most European languages have this word in one form or another: French has *sac*, Italian has *sacco*, Spanish has *saco*, and they are all related to the ancient Greek *sakkos*, which had several meanings. It was applied by the Greeks to almost anything coarse, such as material made of animal (particularly goat) hair, rough cloth, and even bushy beards! Eventually the word evolved to mean not just the material itself but any bags made from it; the first ones are thought to have been 'sacks' used for transporting grain in biblical times. Several Middle Eastern languages have the word *saq*, which the Greeks possibly adapted to fit in with their pronunciation and word structure.

b) There are two possible explanations for the act of 'sacking' a town. The English expression dates from the 1540s and is thought to reflect the French order, given by military commanders to the troops, *mettre à sac* (i.e., 'to put into a sack' anything of value they could find while pillaging a town). The other explanation is that it is derived from the Old Norse *rannsaka*, a combination of *rann* ('house') and *saekja* ('to search'). And this of course is the origin of a closely related word, 'to ransack'.

c) The 'sack' so beloved of Sir John Falstaff in the Shakespearean plays was really *sherris sack* ('dry sherry'), the word 'sack' being related linguistically to the modern French *sec* ('dry') and its Latin equivalent, *siccus*. In the sixteenth and seventeenth centuries dry sherry was a very popular tipple in England, and Sir John would not have been alone in his predilection.

d) 'To give somebody the sack' is an expression dating back to the days when itinerant journeymen (i.e., workers who were employed by the *journée* or 'day') would leave their bag of tools in the care of their clients until the job was completed. However, if the person employing them was dissatisfied with their efforts, he or she would 'give them the sack' of tools and order them off the premises. The expression was first recorded with this meaning in the early nineteenth century.

SAP

Examples: a) The **sap** oozed out of the plant's broken stem.

b) The **saps** were constructed as a defence against the enemy.

a) This is a word with a long history and has linguistic connections with several other European languages. Old English had *sæp*, Old High German had *saf*, and modern German has *Saft* for 'sap' (the juice of a plant). All can be traced back to the Latin *sapa*, a term used by the Romans for new wine that had been boiled until it made a thick, pungent mass. Related words were the noun *sapor* ('taste') and the verb *sapere* ('to taste', 'to have flavour', as well as 'to think'). It is also cognate with the Latin noun *sapientia* ('wisdom') and the adjective *sapiens* ('wise' or 'thinking', as in the term *homo sapiens* ('thinking man')). The connection here is the acknowledgement that 'taste' implies the ability to distinguish between what is good and what is bad or, in other words, to display a degree of discernment; and wisdom similarly implies a facility for deciding what is appropriate or acceptable and what is not. The ancient Romans' realization that there was a strong link between 'taste' and 'wisdom' also explains why in modern Spanish (a Latin-based language) the verb *saber* means both 'to know' and 'to taste of'.

b) 'To sap' as a military term means to dig 'saps' or trenches towards the enemy lines. English borrowed the term from Middle French *saper* 'to undermine' and was used to describe the activities of soldiers ordered to dig trenches beneath enemy walls and fortifications and thus weaken them in the hope that they would collapse. A refinement of the strategy was to convey barrels of gunpowder through the 'saps' and explode them under the fortifications; this was almost guaranteed to hasten their destruction. Such soldiers in the British Army were traditionally known as 'sappers', and prior to 1856 formed the Corps of Royal Sappers and Miners but were eventually amalgamated into the Corps of Royal Engineers. And the most junior rank in the corps is 'sapper', equating to 'private' in other units of the British Army.

The modern French verb was based on the Old French noun *sappe*, a 'digging' or 'trenching' tool, derived from the medieval Latin *sappa* ('spade').

SAW

Examples: a) The carpenter bought an expensive new **saw**.

b) The old lady was always quoting proverbs and old **saws**.

c) I **saw** her walking through the park.

a) The cutting tool recognizable by its blade with a jagged or toothed edge and designed originally for cutting through wood or bringing down trees is generally referred to as a 'saw'. In Old English it was known as *sagu* (*sage* in the oblique cases) and is linguistically related to the Latin *secare* and modern Russian *sekat'*, both of which mean 'to cut'. The Indo-European root here is *sek*, which spawned many cognate words in European languages associated with the act of cutting: a 'saw' in Old Norse was *sög*, modern Swedish has *såg*, and German has *Säge*. The same root is also the origin of the Old English noun *seaxe*, a long knife much favoured by the Germanic tribes who first invaded Britain in the fifth century AD. The distinctive shape of the tool or weapon, inextricably associated with the foreign invaders, meant that they were soon known as 'the people who used the *seaxe*', or, as we now refer to them, 'the Saxons'.

There is also an interesting comparison here with Spanish. The cognate word *sierra* can either refer to the cutting instrument or to a mountain range. From the distance, the outline of a range of mountains can be said to resemble the teeth of a saw.

b) 'Saw' is not used very much now as synonym for 'proverb' or 'adage', but it does survive in older literary texts. Its origin is the Old English *sagu* ('report' or 'account'; Middle English *sawe*), derived from the Old English infinitive *secgan* ('to say'). In other words, 'saw' and its synonym 'saying' are cognate and the former is really nothing more than a variation of the latter. Another relative is the noun 'saga', now used to describe almost any long-running tale but originally a form of narrative entertainment perhaps most closely associated with the Iceland of long ago.

c) As the past tense of the verb 'to see', the word 'saw' was written in Old English as *saeh* and in Middle English as *sauh*. The 'w' of the modern spelling is a remnant of the Old English plural past tense form *sawon*.

SCALE

Examples: a) The final voters tipped the **scale**.

b) Most fish have skin covered in **scales**.

c) He bought himself a large-**scale** map of France.

a) The Old English word in the background here is *scalu* ('shell', 'husk', or 'dish'). Another suggested linguistic connection is with the word 'skull', and this leads to a fascinating if somewhat gruesome association with modern times. Ancient tribes in northern Europe and many other parts of the world frequently recycled human skulls as drinking cups. And the Norsemen's term for such an improvised drinking cup, *skál* (thought to be an earlier form of English 'skull'), explains why the Scandinavian way of proposing a toast is still to lift a cup (or probably a glass in today's world) and utter a hearty '*skál!*' The modern spelling is, of course, '*skol*'.

b) The scales on a fish and other creatures are not unrelated to those mentioned above. They are derived from the Germanic root **skal* ('to peel') and Old High German *skala* ('husk of a fruit' or 'eggshell'). Shells and husks both convey the idea of hard outer protective casing and their similarity to shells found on a seashore did not go unnoticed by primitive peoples. There is also, of course, the figurative use of these hard layers of protective skin which we encounter in the biblical expression 'the scales fell from his eyes'.

c) 'Scale' in the sense of a means of recording increasing or decreasing volume, intensity, measurement, etc., is derived from the Latin *scala* ('ladder') and its related verb *scandere* ('to climb'). An interesting linguistic relative here is the literary technique of 'scanning' verse. The ancient grammarians saw this as a method for measuring verse by considering it foot by foot, much as one would climb a ladder rung by rung.

SCHOOL

Examples: a) He studied hard at **school** and passed all his exams.

b) A **school** of dolphins swam past the little boat.

a) 'School' is used in many languages to define the place where people gather together in order to study and receive instruction: Italian has *scuola*, Spanish *escuela*, Russian *shkola*, German *Schule*, and French (which dropped the 's') *école*.

Even the Celtic languages such as Welsh, Scots Gaelic, and Irish Gaelic have *ysgol*, *sgoil*, and *scoil* respectively. Old English had the word *scol*, a borrowing of the Latin *schola*. And all of these words come from the ancient Greek *skholē*, which, believe it or not, meant 'leisure' or 'idleness'! And there was even a related adverb *skholēi* ('slowly' or 'in a leisurely manner') and a verb *scholazein* ('to have spare time' or 'to be at leisure').

The rather surprising connection between a modern 'school' and Greek words suggesting inactivity is easily explained. Generally speaking, women and slaves in Greek society would work from dawn till dusk, but the youth of the leisured classes would have had time on their hands when they could sit around listening to learned men and indulging in philosophical discussion. And such 'discussion groups' were the forerunners of our 'schools'.

b) A 'school' of fish is of a totally different linguistic history. In Old English the word *scolu* ('crowd' or 'throng') was allied to the Germanic root **skel* ('to divide'). In its present form, the word is thought to have entered English in about 1400 from early Dutch, which had *schole* for a group of fish.

The association with a root suggesting division would appear to be related to the idea that a 'school' of fish is a group that has been 'cut off' or separated from a larger one.

SCORE

Examples: a) The instructions told him to **score** along the dotted line.
　　　　　　 b) He borrowed a **score** from his uncle.

a) The Old English *scoru* was derived from Germanic roots, particularly the Old Norse *skor* ('incision'), a word which lies at the base of many words we still use in modern English such as 'scar', 'shear', and 'score', the modern spelling of *skor*. The original active verb here was *scieran* ('to cut' or 'to cut off'), which shows up in many modern cognates: 'share' (a portion 'cut off' for someone) and 'skirt' or 'shirt' (basically the same words, referring to lengths of cloth 'cut off' from a larger piece). Even 'shore' is a cognate, designating a place where the land has been 'cut off' and now meets the sea.

b) In ancient times there were many societies which employed the vigesimal system of counting certain domestic goods, particularly animals such as sheep and goats. According to this system, the number twenty was used as a mathematical base and a shepherd, for instance, counting his flock would make a notch on a stick every time he reached the twentieth sheep. And around the year 1400 an alternative to the standard *twentig* appeared, *scoru*, a term which has been adopted in modern English as 'score', a frequently heard colloquialism for 'twenty'.

Over the course of time the practice of recording numbers with a visible mark spread out into other areas of activity. Innkeepers, for example, would keep track of how much his customers had drunk by making scratch marks on the table top (or, later, chalk marks on a slate) so that both parties at the end of the evening knew exactly how much ale had to be paid for. In other words, this was the time for 'settling the score', and the expression has now found its way into general use. By the 1670s people taking part in sports and games were using the expression 'to keep score' to record how many points a player had 'notched up'.

The practice of referring to written music as a 'score' dates from the very early eighteenth century. The connection here is thought to be the convention of connecting related staves by 'scores', or lines.

SCOT

Examples: a) He got off **scot**-free.

b) Angus was proud of being a **Scot**.

a) In Anglo-Saxon England, if a man was deemed to be *scotfreo* ('scot-free') it meant that he was exempt from payment of royal taxes. But the word 'scot' in this context had nothing to do with inhabitants of the northernmost part of the British Isles. It is a term dating back to Old Norse *skot*, which had two basic meanings: either something that had been thrown or 'shot' (such as a missile of some description) or a payment. The association between the two is thought to be the practice of 'throwing' monies due onto a table or into a bag, perhaps on set dates throughout the year when land rents became due. The Indo-European root here is **skeud* ('to throw', 'to chase', or 'to shoot').

An associated expression 'scot and lot' (literally 'tax and share') is now mainly of historical interest. It was introduced into England in the thirteenth century as a form of parish or town taxation based solely on a person's ability to pay.

b) The original Scots did not come from Scotland. Accounts vary, but the current consensus of opinion is that the country we think of as Scotland was inhabited by the Picts (i.e., the 'painted' ones) and Gaels (i.e., the 'woodsmen') when the Romans arrived. Their name for the land north of the Antonine Wall, extending from the Firth of Clyde to the Firth of Forth, was Caledonia. The Scoti are thought to have arrived from Ireland in the fourth and fifth centuries AD, and by about the tenth century the term 'Scotia' was appearing in Latin texts to designate the northern parts of Britain inhabited by Gaelic-speaking peoples. The term 'Scotland' did not take root until the Middle Ages.

Things get a little complicated when we look at the Gaelic name for the country, Alba. It is derived from a Celtic name with the Indo-European root *albh* ('white') and borrowed by the ancient Greeks and Romans who referred to the whole of Britain as Albion.

Just to complicate things even more, the historian Geoffrey of Monmouth (c. 1100–c. 1155), the Welsh-born, Oxford-educated historian, along with other writers of the time, applied a modified form of the Gaelic 'Alba' to the northern part of Britain, calling it 'Albania'. This should not be confused with the modern country we now refer to as Albania, which in Albanian is Shqipëri.

SEE

Examples: a) After his cataract operation he could **see** much better.

b) A bishop is responsible for the administration of a **see**.

a) There has been some dispute among linguists over the years about the origin of this word. It used to be thought that it was related to the Indo-European root *sekw* ('to follow') and therefore to the Latin verb *sequor* ('I follow'), but the theory fell out of favour. An alternative theory was proposed suggesting that the closest linguistic relative to the verb 'to see' was 'to say', but neither camp has been able to produce conclusive evidence.

The connection with the root *sek* ('to follow'), however, does appear to be reasonably logical; after all, 'seeing' something implies following it with one's eyes. And it would appear that all the Germanic languages have, like English, adopted the association between seeing and the Latin verb: Old English had *sēon*, Old High German had *sehan*, modern German has *sehen*, Icelandic has *sjá*, Danish has *see*, and Swedish has *se*. On the other hand, the Romance languages took a different route: French has *voir*, Spanish has *ver*, Italian has *vedere*, and these are all descended from the Latin *videre* ('to see'). We can complete the picture by pointing out that the Latin *video* is cognate with the Greek *oida* (and an earlier *woida*), the perfect tense of an archaic verb *eidō* meaning 'I see' which was used in ancient Greek for 'I know'.

b) An ecclesiastical area of administration where a bishop has his seat is known as a 'see', a contracted form of the Latin verb *sedere* ('to sit'). But the associations do not end here. The base from which a bishop governs his see will normally be a cathedral and this is another word with its roots in the idea of sitting, although this time the origin is Greek. 'Cathedral' is formed from two Greek words, *kata* ('down') and *hezesthai* ('to sit'), which when run together produce *kathezesthai* ('to sit down'). The resulting noun, *kathedra*, therefore means nothing more than 'chair'. Consequently, a 'cathedral', as we now understand the word, would have been merely a place where the bishop kept his 'seat', a symbol of his elevated position and authority. This is fitting symbolism when we remember that the word 'bishop' is itself the contraction of two more Greek words *epi* ('over') and *skopein* ('to look'), and so his principal task is to 'oversee' (the Latin equivalent gave us 'to supervise') the business of the diocese. In the secular world the association with 'sitting' can be seen today when we talk of university professors 'having the chair' in French, English Literature, or Molecular Physics. And a perfect link between church and laity can be seen in Spanish, which has *catedral* for cathedral but uses the term *catedrático* for a university professor.

SHAMBLES

Examples: a) The room was a total **shambles** after the party.

b) He **shambles** along like an old man.

a) Old English had *sceamol* and Middle English had *schamel* which both simply meant 'bench' and are derived from the Latin *scamellum* ('bench' or 'stool'), the diminutive form of *scamnum* ('step' or 'stool'). To complete the picture, however, we have to go back to the Greek *skēptein* ('to support') and its reflexive form *skēptesthai* ('to support oneself'), usually with a *skēptron* ('stick'). By the fourteenth century 'shambles' had become the specific term for meat and fish markets where butchers and fishmongers displayed their wares on 'benches', rather than simply spreading them on the ground.

The 1540s saw something of a change in meaning and the word was applied to the establishment where animals were slaughtered rather than where their flesh was sold. As these were always messy places with blood, bones, and carcasses lying all over the floor, they soon became synonymous with carnage and hideous disorder. As far as we know, the word 'shambles' was first used to describe general disarray and confusion in 1901.

b) It has been suggested that 'to shamble' is related to the Old French and Italian verbs *escamper* and *scampare* respectively, meaning 'to decamp' or 'to escape'. These verbs were derived in turn from the Latin *ex* ('out of') and *campus* ('field' or 'theatre of action'), thus suggesting flight from a battle or out of captivity at some speed. But this does not tie in with the impression of a man or woman 'shambling' along.

Another, more plausible, explanation is that 'shambling' is a shortened form of the descriptive phrase 'shamble legs' (i.e., having legs resembling wobbly, unstable trestles or table legs). Anyone compared to such an item of furniture would look unsteady and hesitant in his or her movements and gait; this is almost a perfect description of anyone 'shambling' along.

SHED

Examples: a) Trees **shed** their leaves in the autumn.

b) He had a little **shed** at the bottom of his garden.

a) The basic idea behind the word 'shed' is separation. Old English had *sceadan* ('to divide' or 'to separate'; with an additional meaning of 'to scatter'), derived from the Proto-Germanic root **skaith* ('a divide' or 'a split'), which is related to the Greek *skhizein* ('to split'). And this word, of course, has produced many off-shoots currently in use in modern English. A 'schism' occurs when the whole divides into rival factions; a 'watershed' divides two bodies of water but also has the figurative meaning of a dividing line or turning point; and 'scissors' take their name from the cognate Latin verb *scindere* ('to cut').

But there are also two cognates which require a fuller explanation. The Norwegian word *ski*, now adopted into many languages, is derived from the Old Norse word *skith* ('snow shoe'), the original meaning of which was a 'a strip of wood split off from a larger one'.

'Science' is also a noun with probable origins in the concept of 'splitting off'. We now apply the word to learning or knowledge acquired by study. It came into English from the Latin noun *scientia* ('knowledge') and the verb *scire* ('to know'). The basic meaning of the word, however, is something along the lines of 'those things known, as opposed to (or 'separated' from) those things which are unknown'.

b) The little hut or outbuilding we refer to as a 'shed' is so called because it tends to be poorly lit and dark. It is really just a variant of the words 'shade' and 'shadow'.

The Old English for a 'shed' was *scead*, directly related to another Old English word *sceadu* ('shade', 'darkness', or 'arbour'), and this is directly related to the ancient Greek word *skotos* ('darkness' or 'gloom').

SLEDGE

Examples: a) She came down the hill on a wooden **sledge**.

b) Tom smashed the rocks with a **sledge**hammer.

a) 'Sledge', 'sleigh', and 'sled' are all variants of the same word. 'Sledge' is thought to been originally spelled 'sleds' and served as the plural of 'sled'. This word was not known in Old English and made its appearance only in the seventeenth century; 'sledge' (or sleds) was probably a borrowing from the Dutch dialect form *sleedse*.

They are all closely related to, if not directly descended from, the Old English *slīdan*, from which we derive the modern verb 'to slide'. This is directly related to the Greek *olisthos* ('slippery'), from the Sanskrit *srí* ('to flow').

A further surprising linguistic connection is the modern Russian *sled* ('track') and the related verb *sledovat'* ('to follow'). The original meaning of this verb seems to have been 'to walk in the tracks of'.

b) The compound noun 'sledgehammer' is tautological, as the Old English word *slecg* (pronounced 'sledge') meant 'hammer'. Old Norse had *sleggja* ('hammer'), which was related to the noun *slege* ('a beating'). Both are cognate with the Old English verb *slean*, which has two derivatives in modern English: 'to slay' and 'to slaughter'.

The second part of the word (i.e., 'hammer') can be considered a literal remnant of the Stone Age; Old English had *hamor* or *hamer* and Old Norse had *hamarr*. *Hamarr* referred not only to the implement used to smash stones but to the stones themselves, since a secondary meaning of *hamarr* was 'crag' or 'rock'. Another example of the linguistic fusion between the tool and its intended target has a parallel in other languages: ancient Greek had *akmōn* ('anvil', originally made of stone, no doubt), which is cognate with the modern Russian *kamen'* ('stone' or 'rock').

A likely explanation for the connection is that the original Stone Age hammer was little more than a lump of stone attached to a crude wooden handle; the hammer and anvil, therefore, essentially comprised the same material.

SMART

Examples: a) He had eyestrain and his eyes were beginning to **smart**.
b) She looked very **smart** in her new uniform.
c) The **smart** money is on the favourite to win at Aintree.

a) The use of the word 'smart' to denote a short, sharp pain goes back a long way in the linguistic history of English. In Anglo-Saxon times the word *smeart* meant 'causing a sharp pain', and this is still evident in its nearest modern counterpart, the German *schmerzen* ('to hurt' or 'to cause pain'). If we go further back, we find that it is also related to the Latin *mordere* ('to bite'), a word which has also given us the expression 'a mordant (i.e., 'biting') sense of humour'. Travelling yet further back in time we find that *mordere* and 'to smart' are both related to the Greek adjective *smerdnos* ('awful').

b) In the eleventh or twelfth century the concepts of biting and transience associated with a 'smart' pain were transferred to descriptions of a person's sense of humour and quickness of wit. The word therefore became associated with intelligence and intelligent people tended to enjoy greater social and personal success. As a result, they would be more likely to earn more and be able to afford fashionable, well-cut, and no doubt expensive clothes. In other words, they would not only sound witty and clever but would look more attractive and 'smart'.

c) To know where 'the smart money' is implies that an investor has insider knowledge or is at least very well informed about where to take a risk or to place money to be sure of maximizing his financial gains. But this was not always the case. In the seventeenth century soldiers, sailors, and ordinary workmen could be granted 'smart money' if they were injured or fell ill whilst performing their duties and so could not work. In other words, the original 'smart' money was a precursor to the modern concept of sickness benefits or compensation for injuries sustained at work.

SMASHING

Examples: a) The child began **smashing** all his toys.
           b) We had a **smashing** time at Jim's party.

a) 'Smashing', 'bashing', and 'crashing' are largely onomatopoeic words imitating the sound associated with a particular destructive activity. Etymologists do not seem to have been able to identify a specific linguistic origin, although Norwegian *smaska* ('to break to bits') is almost certainly related. Possibly, 'smashing' was a word introduced to English by the Vikings, but we cannot be absolutely certain.

b) If you want to find out why 'smashing' can be a synonym for 'excellent', there is not much point in looking in an English dictionary. Most (even the most authoritative ones) will probably tell you that it is simply a slang expression and that the reason for such usage is unknown.

But there is one distinctly plausible explanation. After the Great Famine in Ireland in the nineteenth century, thousands of Irishmen and their families settled in England, particularly in and around Liverpool. Many of these people were Irish Gaelic–speaking and after a time some of their words and expressions were adopted (and adapted) by the local populace. One such expression could well have been *is maith sin* ('that is good'; pronounced 'smaashin'). Its phonetic similarity to an existing English word would have aided its easy assimilation into the language.

Until a couple of decades or so ago, a man or woman might have been described colloquially as 'a smasher', and again this had nothing to do with what might have been his or her employment in the demolition industry. It simply meant that he or she was very good looking and is no doubt also related to the Irish Gaelic expression.

A few other Irish Gaelic words which entered English at the same time include *cailín* ('girl'; anglicized 'colleen'), *bróg* ('shoe'; anglicized 'brogue'), and, of course, *uisce* ('water'; anglicized 'whiskey'). This last example might just as well have come from Scots Gaelic, which also has *uisce* for water but is anglicized 'whisky'.

SOIL

Examples: a) This **soil** is good for growing vegetables and flowers.

b) His mother told him not to **soil** his clean shirt.

a) It's quite understandable to assume that the meanings of the word 'soil' share a common ancestor, but in fact they do not. When we use the word as a synonym for the friable earth in which we grow plants and vegetables, we are attributing to it a meaning which it has only enjoyed since the early fourteenth century. Prior to that, it had the more general meaning of 'land' or 'country' as can be seen in the surviving expression 'native soil'.

The origin of this word is the Latin *solum*, which referred to the lowest part of anything, including the ground and also the underside or 'sole' of the foot. A derivative of the latter meaning was *solea* ('sandal'), which because of its resemblance to a certain flatfish also provided the name by which it is known in English, the 'sole'.

b) In Old English the word *syl* (or *sol*) was applied to any muddy, filthy patch of land where pigs wallowed. In Middle English the word evolved into *soile* (alternatively *soyle*), a spelling which is recognizably connected with the form of the word as we know it today.

However it was spelled, the derivation of the word is the Latin *sus* ('pig'; cognate with the Old English *sū*, the origin of modern English 'sow') and the diminutive form *suculus* ('piglet').

The best indicator, however, of how the word changed its meaning is provided by French. Old French had *souil* ('pigsty') and the related verb *soillier*, which originally simply meant 'to wallow' and only acquired the meaning of 'to make dirty' at a later stage. It was not until the seventeenth century that 'soil' in English could be applied generally to excrement and filth.

The Latin term for the humble pig and piglet are also thought to be the origin of the associated verb 'to sully', now mainly used in figurative expressions such as 'to sully one's reputation' or 'to sully one's hands' (i.e., in shameful or unlawful activities).

SOUND

Examples: a) She was so deaf that she could not hear a **sound**.
            b) He was judged to be of **sound** mind.
            c) They crossed Plymouth **Sound** in a dinghy.
            d) Jim decided to **sound** the river so as not to run aground.

a) The English word 'sound' evolved from the Old French *son* and Latin *sonus*, both of which can trace their origins back to the Sanskrit word *svanati* ('it makes a noise'). Interestingly, the same Sanskrit word also produced the English word 'swan', the bird renowned for the particularly raucous noise it makes when annoyed. Another linguistic relative here is the Italian *sonata* (literally 'sounded'), used to denote music produced on an instrument as opposed to *cantata* (literally 'sung') music produced by the voice.

b) As an adjective, 'sound' can be used to describe an object or person in good condition, undamaged, or uninjured. It is derived from the Old English *sund*, which is related to the Latin *sanus* ('healthy'). And *sanus* shows up, of course, in another English word: 'sane', now almost exclusively applied to someone whose mind is considered to be functioning correctly. The Old English *sund* is cognate with the modern German adjective *gesund* ('healthy') and the noun *Gesundheit* ('health'). The Latin *sanus* is also heard in the maxim bequeathed to us by the Latin author Juvenal, *mens sana in corpore sano* ('a healthy mind in a healthy body').

c) As a geographical term dating back to the fourteenth century, a 'sound' is a narrow strait in which the waters are relatively calm and sheltered and therefore safe to swim in. And this is the clue to the etymology of the word; it is a relative of the verb 'to swim'. In Old English *sund* meant both 'sea' and 'swimming'.

d) When we talk about 'sounding' or 'assessing the depth' of water there is a clear relationship to the noun *sund*, and another Old English word *sundgyrd* or *sundgierd* ('sounding pole', i.e., a pole used to prod the bottom of a river to see how much clearance a boat has).

SPADE

Examples: a) He needed to dig a hole but could not find his **spade**.

b) The pack of cards was missing the ace of **spades**.

a) The Old English *spadu* and modern English 'spade' are both cognate with the Greek *spathē*, which had several meanings but generally referred to any flat piece of wood or metal. It was basically a weaver's term for the instrument used when beating down the threads of the woof in order to keep the fabric tight. But it was also a Greek soldier's term for his 'broadsword', which, when not being used to kill people, would have doubled up as an instrument for digging holes, trenches, and possibly even graves. By the time the word made its way into English the tool's function had become more specific and the military connection had been lost. A 'spade' was now simply a digging tool.

If we say that somebody 'calls a spade a spade' when we mean that that person is a blunt speaker, we are perpetuating a mistranslation. The original Greek expression was *tēn skaphēn skaphēn legein* (literally 'to call a bowl a bowl'). It appears, however, that when Erasmus (1466–1536) was translating the Greek he confused *skaphē* ('a bowl') with *spathē* 'a spade' and the error has persisted.

b) There is much discussion and plenty of disagreement about the origins of card games in Europe. One point where all historians seem to agree, however, is that the suit we refer to as 'spades' has nothing to do with excavating the earth. The 'spade' in question here is directly descended from the Italian *spada* ('sword'). Modern Spanish has a cognate word for 'sword', *espada*, and on Spanish playing cards the image of a 'spade' is far more clearly identifiable as a weapon of war than its modern British counterpart. The military connection is further evidenced by the French for this suit of cards, *pique*, a weapon of war known in English as a 'pike'.

The immediate antecedent of the Italian and Spanish terms is the Latin *spatha* (cognate with the Greek *spathē*), a broad, two-edged sword without a point as well as the term for a kitchen utensil used for mixing or stirring. A further cognate here is the Greek for a eunuch, *spadōn*, a word linked linguistically to the modern English veterinary term 'to spay'.

SPELL

Examples: a) The teacher asked her to **spell** the word aloud.
b) John found a magic **spell** in a book about wizards.
c) He went to work in Glasgow for a **spell**.

a) The Indo-European root *spel* ('to say aloud' or 'to recite') produced a vast array of words in various languages, most of which connected in some way with the act of speaking. In Old English *spellian* meant 'to tell', 'to speak', or 'to talk', and the extended meaning of 'naming individual letters of a word' entered English around 1400 from the Old French *espeler* ('to explain', 'to interpret', or simply 'to read aloud').

b) It was not until the sixteenth century that 'spell' acquired the meaning of a magical and usually malicious incantation frequently pronounced in incomprehensible words or sentences. Earlier on, from around 1200, it defined any string of words and really meant nothing more than an utterance or statement. Another cognate word, perhaps surprisingly, is 'gospel'. It has almost exclusively theological connotations now, but it was originally just another way of saying 'good news', a literal translation of the biblical Greek *euaggelia* (from *eu* ('good') and *aggelia* ('message'); more recognizable perhaps as the word behind the term 'evangelical').

c) The use of 'spell' to define or refer to a period of time is an interesting one and involves a complete reversal of the original meaning. In Old English *spelian* meant 'to substitute' or 'to take someone else's place' and was used particularly in occupations where work was organized into periods of what we would now refer to as 'shifts'. This was very common, for instance, at sea, where a sailor at the end of his watch would be relieved and given time for relaxation, which might have involved playing games of some description. The substitute was known in Old English as the *gespelia*, a word of uncertain origin but probably related to *spilian* ('to play'), a linguistic relative of the modern German verb with the same meaning, *spielen*.

By the eighteenth century the idea of substitution had faded somewhat and the associated noun now referred to the time spent relaxing as opposed to the form of relaxation itself.

SPRUCE

Examples: a) The needles of the **spruce** tree are particularly sharp.

b) He was looking very **spruce** in his new suit.

a) The term 'spruce' for the particular type of coniferous tree that originates from the Baltic area has been used in English since the middle of the seventeenth century. It takes its name from the region known as Prussia which, at one stage, was the most important state in the German empire. Its original inhabitants were not Germanic, as can be seen by the fact that the language known as Old Prussian is more akin to Lithuanian than it is to German.

Linguists have puzzled over the appearance of the initial letter 's' of 'spruce' if the derivation of the word really is Prussia; one distinctly plausible suggestion is that the English word is a borrowing from Polish. The Polish for Prussia is *Prusy* and the phrase *z Prus* (which would have sounded like 'spruce' to English ears) means 'from Prussia'.

b) During the Middle Ages the Hanseatic League, centred around the Baltic countries, enjoyed a reputation for goods of fine quality. One commodity in particular for which there was great demand throughout Europe was leather; Elizabethan jerkins were frequently made out of leather imported from Prussia into England from about 1400 and known as 'spruce leather'. As it was virtually a byword for quality, if not sheer luxury, any young man seen sporting such a garment was said to look very presentable in his 'spruce' jerkin. Since about 1580 'spruce' has described the wearer's appearance rather than the garment's origin.

STERN

Examples: a) As a teacher, he was known to be very **stern**.

b) The rear end of a ship is known as the **stern**.

a) The Old English form of the adjective 'stern' was *styrne*, which was derived from the Proto-Germanic root **sternijaz* and has cognate forms *starr* ('stiff') and *störrig* ('obstinate') in modern German. A modern English verb which also has strong etymological links with the word is 'to stare'. After all, if we 'stare' at somebody we look at them with a 'firm' and 'rigid' gaze, and this is often interpreted by others as firmness of character if not downright obstinacy and rigidity.

Another cognate which seems a little remote but is nonetheless related is the now frequently used prefix 'stereo-'. This can be traced all the way back to ancient Greek which had *stereos* ('rigid' or 'stiff'). It was also used by the Greeks to express solidity and cubic measures, such as in the expression *stereos arithmos* ('a cubed number'), and this concept of three-dimensional measurement is the origin of words now used in English such as 'stereophonic' and 'stereoscopic'.

b) The Old Norse term *stjorn* ('stern') was directly related to the Old English *stēoran* ('to steer'), the relationship between the two being that ships, boats, etc., have always been steered from the rear, or, as we now refer to it, the 'stern'. By comparison, the Romans referred to this part of a ship as the *puppis* (of unknown etymology), which has given us another nautical expression, the 'poop deck'.

A further Old Norse term with strong connections to the skills involved in navigation is the verb *styra* ('to guide'). It has an interesting linguistic history as it gives us a very convincing clue as to the manner in which steering was achieved in ancient times. The Old Norse verb provided the Anglo-Saxons with the noun *stēor* ('rudder'), a relative of an Old Norse noun *staurr* ('pole'), which is cognate with the Greek *stauros* (also 'pole'). It would appear that, for the ancients, steering a boat involved little more than pushing a pole into the river bed, much in the same way as punters do even today.

STILL

Examples: a) He stood **still** in the hope that he would not be noticed.

b) 'I'm not sure if he is **still** here,' said his secretary.

c) They had a **still** in the loft where they made illicit booze.

a) If we compare the use of the adjective 'still' in English with the German *still* ('silent'), we see that the concepts of stillness and silence have long shared a close semantic relationship. For instance, the German Christmas carol 'Stille Nacht' is rendered in English as 'Silent Night', but both titles convey the idea of a night-time when all is quiet and not a sound is heard. The confusion here has obviously come about because most things that stand 'still' make no noise; motion generates sound. But for an even more convincing illustration of the link between lack of movement and silence, we only have to think of the Latin verb *silere*, meaning both 'to remain motionless' and 'not to make a sound'. And this is the origin of the English word 'silence'.

b) The adverb of time 'still' is really just a temporal equivalent of 'still' meaning 'motionless'. If we say that an event is 'still' continuing, or that someone is 'still' here, the same basic idea applies, but now the reference is to time as opposed to space.

c) On the other hand, when we talk about a 'still' as a mechanism for producing alcoholic liquor the origin of the word and its linguistic associations are totally different. 'Still' in this sense is from the Latin verb *distillare* ('to fall in little drops'), the derivative noun here being *stilla* ('a drop'). The verb *stillen* ('to distil') was used in Middle English from about 1300, and the apparatus used in such a process came to be known as a 'still' at some time in the 1530s.

STOCK

Examples: a) He comes from very good **stock**.

b) James made a lot of money dabbling in **stocks** and shares.

c) The family sold up lock, **stock**, and barrel.

d) She has a new novel on the **stocks**.

e) He keeps a good **stock** of pencils in his drawer.

a) The basic idea of this word is tree trunk. It comes from an ancient Germanic root **stukkaz* ('tree trunk'), and entered modern English via Old English *stoc* or *stocc*, ultimately linked with the Greek *stupos* ('stem', 'stump', or 'stick'). The use of the noun 'stock' in the context of family bloodlines is purely figurative and dates from the fourteenth century. Direct lineage is represented by the 'trunk' of a tree and the other family relationships by its branches.

b) In the early days of banking it was quite common for borrowers and lenders to make use of a tally stick to keep a record of financial transactions. This involved cutting notches in the stick, slicing it lengthways into two parts, and each party to the transaction keeping one half. One of the halves, however, was longer than the other, and this was kept by the man who lent the money. This half was then known as 'the stock', and the person who retained it became the 'stockholder'. Many words and expressions followed: stockbroker, stock market, stock exchange, etc.

c) To say 'lock, stock, and barrel' when referring to the whole of anything is to borrow the names of the constituent parts of an old firearm, the flintlock musket. The 'lock' was the part that held the flint which produced the spark that ignited the gunpowder; the 'stock' was the heavy part of the gun that was held firmly against the shoulder; and the 'barrel', of course, was the tube out of which the musket ball was fired.

d) It was the craft of boatbuilding that gave us the expression 'on the stocks' for when we mean that a project is in the advanced stages of preparation. The 'stocks', in this case, were originally lengths of wood used to prop up a boat while it was under construction. It had found its way into common parlance by the late fifteenth century.

e) Keeping a 'stock' of anything is thought to be a reference to keeping stuff in reserve in what originally would have been a container made of wood (possibly a hollowed-out tree stump). By extension, it came to be applied to anything in reserve, such as the liquid we refer to as chicken or beef 'stock', which in former times guaranteed that when meat was scarce there was always the wherewithal for making vegetable soup, if nothing else. This usage dates from the mid-eighteenth century.

STRAND

Examples: a) Jim and Jane walked along the **strand** holding hands.
           b) They extracted the DNA from a single **strand** of hair.

a) The word 'strand' survives now mainly in poetry and in some place names, such as 'the Strand' in London, so named in 1246. In former times, however, it was commonly used for what we should now refer to as the 'shore' or even 'beach'. The Indo-European root behind it is *ster* ('to stretch out'), which has spawned quite a number of surprising cognates in various European languages. Old English and Middle English had *strand*, Middle Low German had *strant*, and modern German has *Strand* for 'beach'. Russian has the cognate noun *strana* meaning 'country'. This might appear unrelated to 'shore' until we compare the Indo-European root with the vast 'stretched-out' look of the Russian landscape.

The Greek and Latin related verbs are *storesai* and *sternere* respectively (both meaning 'to spread out' or 'to scatter'), descendants of which include 'straw' (vegetable matter 'strewn' on the ground) and 'street', a thoroughfare made from stones, broken rocks, etc., 'scattered' over earth.

The verb 'to strand' a boat, sailor, etc., on the shore appeared in English in the seventeenth century, and the figurative meaning of leaving somebody in a desperate situation was first attested in 1837.

b) The idea of a single hair or thread being defined as a 'strand' follows a linguistic track which leads back to Roman times and is thematically linked to early Celtic society. The Old French *estran* was derived from the Old High German *streno*, both of which meant 'skein' (a quantity of coiled or knotted yarn, wool, or silk). These nouns are almost certainly related to the Latin *stria* ('furrow' or 'groove'), possibly a reference to a channel of some description in which the 'strands' were laid before being twisted into rope, cord, etc.

The Celtic dimension reappears in the derivation of the word 'skein'. In Scots Gaelic *sgeinnigh* was 'hemp' or 'flax' (in modern Scots Gaelic it denotes a 'fisherman's line') and in Irish Gaelic the word for a 'skein of thread' is *sgainne* or *scainne*. There is also a strong possibility that both of these are connected with Greek *skhoinos* meaning (i) reed, (ii) rushes, or (iii) anything twisted or plaited such as rope, cord, string, etc.

STUD

Examples: a) The builder divided the room with a **stud** wall.
b) She bought the horse from the local **stud** farm.

a) By the thirteenth century the word 'stud' in England had acquired the meaning of 'nail head' and had come to be associated with almost any button-like implement designed for securing or holding an object in place. In Old English the word was *studu* and meant 'pillar', 'prop', or 'post'. Its Germanic root, **stud*, was derived from the Indo-European **stu/sta*, the root behind words such as the Latin *stare* ('to stand'), the Greek *stulos* ('pillar'), and the modern German verb *stützen* ('to prop up' or 'to support'). In more recent times it is also the reason why we refer to a 'stud' wall, meaning a wall constructed by nailing panels to 'studding', or pillars (usually wooden), fixed or secured to a solid base.

Not too long ago, before shirts were manufactured with integral collars, men would keep a stock of 'studs' (small devices specifically designed to attach collars to the rest of the shirt) as part of their wardrobe.

b) The connection between a 'stud' farm and a length of wood used as a means of support might not appear immediately obvious, but nevertheless the two are linguistically related. In Old English the word *stod* (also from the root **sta*) referred to a herd of horses and then came to designate the patch of land where stallions and mares 'stood' before mating. Interestingly, the word 'stallion' is also cognate as it refers, strictly speaking, to male horses that have been kept in a 'stall' until they can be introduced to a mare for breeding. And the German for 'mare', *Stute*, is another derivative of the Indo-European root **sta*.

Since the end of the nineteenth century the word 'stud' has also been applied to priapic young men (presumably by analogy with the activities associated with a 'stud' farm) and since about 1930 it has been used colloquially as a term for any adolescent male.

STY

Examples: a) Farmers usually keep pigs in a **sty**.

b) The doctor said that her **sty** was due to an infection.

a) The use of the word 'sty' to denote a chaotic mess or filthy accommodation dates from the late sixteenth century. In Anglo-Saxon times, however, *stig* was applied to an enclosure used by any domestic animals, not solely pigs; it acquired the narrower meaning of a 'pen for swine' only in the thirteenth century. It was probably about this time also that a new term entered English, *stigwaerd*, the *waerd* or 'ward' charged with making sure that the pigs in the *stig* were well looked after and regularly fed. And *stigwaerd* eventually evolved into the word we recognise today as 'steward' as well as the name Stewart (or its alternative French form, Stuart).

b) The irritating medical condition known as a 'sty' (alternatively spelled 'stye') is from the Anglo-Saxon *stigend eage* ('rising eye') because of the swelling which inevitably accompanies the infection. The verb from which *stigend* is derived is *stigan* ('to rise' or 'to climb'), and this is cognate with other modern English words such as 'stair' (a device for climbing) and 'stirrup', a corruption of the Anglo-Saxon *stig-rap* (originally a rope used when a rider needed to 'climb' up onto his horse). And a 'stile', of course, is a barrier that has to be 'climbed'.

The strange thing is that both kinds of sty can be traced back linguistically to the Indo-European root **stigh*, which is always associated with climbing or moving to a higher level. Its association with a 'rising' pimple on the eyelid is understandable, but why the same root should give us a pen for containing swine is not so obvious; possibly the first pigsties were always situated on higher ground. On the other hand, a clue may lie in the analysis of another cognate Old English noun: *stigolhamm*. This was the term for 'pastureland that could only be entered via a stile', comprising *stigol* ('stile') and *hamm* ('enclosure'). Quite possibly such patches of land were the first 'sties'.

SWALLOW

Examples: a) The **swallow** can be identified by its forked tail.

b) The medicine was very difficult to **swallow**.

a) The etymology of the bird known in English as a 'swallow' is fairly straight-forward, but when we look at the cognates in other languages the situation becomes a little more complicated.

Old English had *swalwe*, derived from the Proto-Germanic root **swalwon* and the Indo-European **swol* ('to move quickly'), an apt etymology considering the speed with which this bird can fly.

Some linguists have claimed that 'swallow' is related to the Greek *alkuōn*, ('kingfisher'), but this seems unlikely. *Alkuōn* is derived from two Greek nouns, *hals* ('the sea') and *kuōn* ('conceiving'), since, according to tradition, the bird hatches its eggs at sea when the weather is calm. In other words, it breeds during the 'halcyon days'.

Another theory is that 'swallow' is linked linguistically to the Russian *solovei* 'nightingale' and the Old Church Slavonic root **solv* ('grey').

But a third theory suggests that it is derived from the Indo-European root **sel/*sol* ('to jump'), which could be a reference to the manner in which the swallow attempts to skip or hop along the ground. If this is correct, then there is a direct link also with the Latin and Greek verbs *salire* and *hallesthai*, which both mean 'to spring', 'to leap', or 'to jump'.

b) The verb 'to swallow' simply means to convey liquid or food from the mouth to the stomach via the throat. It appears to be a purely Germanic word, related to the Old English *swelgan*, derived from the Proto-Germanic **swelgan*, which in turn can be seen in other words of Germanic origin: Old English had *geswelg* or *swelgend* ('gulf' 'abyss'); Old Norse had *svelgr* ('whirlpool' or 'devourer'); and Old High German had *swelgo* ('glutton'). The last example survives in the modern German *schwelgen* ('to overindulge').

TAR

Examples: a) On hot days the **tar** used to melt on the roads.

b) He was a jolly old **tar** who could sing many a fine shanty.

a) The ancient Greeks knew how to extract the sticky, resinous substance we call 'tar' from certain trees, particularly pine. Their term for it was *pissa* (cognate with 'pine' and 'pitch'), but 'tar' (in Old English *teoru* or *teru*) is linguistically linked with modern English 'tree' as well as quite a few words in other European languages. The Indo-European root here is **derw/*dreu* which gave us the generic word 'tree' and also produced the Greek *drus* and Welsh *derwen*, both of which specifically mean 'oak tree'.

Some other cognates and linguistic associations here are totally unexpected. For instance: (i) the Welsh *derwen* produced *derwydd* ('Druid'; i.e., people who recognized the oak for religious purposes) and (ii) the word 'true' (i.e., something firm, solid, and dependable as symbolized by a mighty tree).

A little further afield the cognate Russian word *derevo* ('tree') is also closely related to *zdorov'e* ('health'). The ancient Slavs obviously regarded trees as symbols of power and good health much in the same way that the Romans did; the Latin for oak, *robur*, gave us the word 'robust'.

The tar we spread on roads to produce smooth surfaces is sometimes referred to as 'tarmac'. This is an abbreviation of 'tarmacadam', a word which combines 'tar' with 'McAdam', after John L. McAdam (1756–1836), the Scottish civil engineer who devised the method of improving the nation's highways.

b) Sailors have been affectionately referred to as 'Jack Tars' since about the 1670s. The epithet is a reference to their habit of wearing tarpaulin clothing whenever possible in order to keep dry. The word 'tarpaulin' is thought to have first appeared (as tarpawlin) around 1600 and was created by taking the word 'tar' and combining it with the Latin *pallium* ('a coverlet' or 'Greek cloak'). This same Latin word also gave us 'pall' principally applied now to the cloth used to drape a coffin. And pall-bearers, the people who carry the coffin at a funeral, were originally so called because they held the corners of the 'pall' as a mark of respect for the dear departed.

TATTOO

Examples: a) The sailor had a **tattoo** of a parrot on his arm.

b) The whole family went up to see the Edinburgh **tattoo**.

a) Not so very long ago it was only men who wore tattoos on various parts of their anatomy, and parrot designs were very popular, as were the names of sweethearts. The latter choice, however, could sometimes cause embarrassment if the lady in a man's life suddenly changed, unless by some stroke of luck his new girlfriend had the same name as the old one! Traditionally, sailors were particularly fond of tattoos and this is a clue to the origin of both the practice and the word. The seamen of yore who sought fortune and adventure in the South Seas (an old term for the Pacific) must have visited many of the islands in that part of the world. And one such island would have been Tahiti, where the word for a drawing on the skin was *tatau*. This would have been learned and brought back home by the sailors, but when it was absorbed into English the spelling was changed to 'tattoo'.

b) The military displays we now refer to as 'tattoos' are from a very different source. In the seventeenth century this use of the word was absorbed into English from Dutch, which had the military expression *tap to* ('close the taps'). This was an order that went out every night to announce to the tavern owners that it was time to close the taps (i.e., stop selling liquor to the troops as it was approaching the time for 'lights out'). As the soldiers were returning to barracks, no doubt somewhat the worse for wear, they would have marched to the sound of bugles and the beating of drums. By the time the practice crossed the sea to England, the signal to close the inns was forgotten, but the idea of soldiers marching to the accompaniment of martial music remains with us today.

There is an associated expression, not often heard these days, but which was once fairly common: 'to beat the Devil's tattoo' meant to sit idly and drum the table with one's fingers.

TEMPLE

Examples: a) The ancient Greeks had a **temple** at Delphi.

b) He was killed when the cricket ball hit him on the **temple**.

a) Many religions refer to their places of worship as 'temples' but the origin of the term lies in the ancient Greek verb *temnein* ('to cut'; from the Indo-European root **tem* ('to cut')). The reference here is to a plot of land, 'cut away' from its surrounding area and reserved for a building dedicated to prayer, worship, and quiet contemplation. The Greeks had a related term, *temenos* ('an area of land sacred to the Gods').

Most European languages have also borrowed the original Latin *templum*, even if in slightly varied forms: Italian has *tempio*, Spanish has *templo*, and German *Tempel*. French, however, has a rather odd additional usage: *temple* designates both a 'temple' and a 'church attended by Protestants'.

Curiously, two of the Inns of Court in England are also referred to as 'temples': the Inner Temple and Middle Temple; the explanation for this is both religious and historical. The site which they now occupy was originally the property of the Knights Templar, a body of armed men whose role in the twelfth century was to defend Solomon's Temple in Jerusalem.

b) The word 'temple' referring to those parts of the head found at either side of the forehead is a descendant of *tempula*, a Vulgar Latin variation of the word *tempora* (plural of *tempus* ('time'); from the Indo-European root **ten* or **temp* ('to stretch')). There is some discussion among etymologists as to why this part of the body should have 'temporal' associations, but there are those who believe that the connection is purely martial. The anatomical 'temple' is considered the most fragile part of the skull and a heavy blow to it can have serious, and possibly fatal, consequences. To put it another way, anyone suffering a blow to that part of his head could easily find that the 'time' he has left in this world is very limited.

Another, and perhaps more plausible explanation, however, is that the 'temple' is the part of the head where the skin is at its 'thinnest', a word derived from the Indo-European root **ten* or **temp* ('to stretch').

TIDE

Examples: a) 'Yule**tide**' is an old-fashioned term for Christmas.

b) The **tide** came in so fast they were cut off from the land.

a) In ancient times the movement of the seas must have served as a powerful metaphor for the passage of time, and this has understandably led to a certain degree of linguistic confusion. In Old English *tíd* did not mean 'tide' but 'time', just as do modern Danish *tid* and German *Zeit*, which are all derived from the Indo-European root **di/*da* ('to divide'). So time, etymologically speaking, is what 'divides' our lives into years, months, weeks, and days.

The Old English *tíd* also survives in English archaisms such as 'eventide', 'Whitsuntide', and 'noontide'. It is also clearly seen in the tautological expression

'Time and tide wait for no man', where 'tide' has nothing to do with the sea but is merely a synonym for 'time'.

A modern cognate here is the word 'tidy', which originally had no spatial connotations but meant 'punctual' or 'on time'. Its application to the condition of a room dates from the thirteenth century.

A further development of the Old English *tíd* was *tiding*, literally meaning something which happened or happens at a specific point in time. This meaning was extended to include reports of such events, hence another archaic, but still extant, sense of the word: 'tidings' meaning 'news'. A further development of the Old English term produced *tídan* ('to happen'; i.e., occur at some point in time), which, by the thirteenth century, had become *betide*. And this survives in the modern warning 'woe betide him if . . .' which is simply an older form of saying 'may grief happen to him if . . .'.

b) It was not until the mid-fourteenth century that the word 'tide' was applied to the constant movement of the sea. Prior to that, the Old English expressions *flod* and *ebba* ('flow' and 'retreat') had sufficed to convey the same idea.

The noun *flod* was derived from the Germanic root **flō*, the same root that gave us words such as 'fleet' and 'flood', and *ebba* can be traced back to the Latin and Greek prepositions *ab* and *apo*, both of which mean 'away from'. So the 'ebb tide' in modern English simply describes the waters as they 'flow away' from the shoreline.

TILL

Examples: a) I'll wait for you **till** nine o'clock but no later.

b) Every day he would **till** the land for about three hours.

c) The robber demanded all the money in the **till**.

a) This word, with some slight variations of spelling, exists in all the Scandinavian languages. The form 'till' in English is now seen as an abbreviation of 'until', which in fact was a later development ('til' is found in Old English; 'until' appeared c. 1200) and is tautological: the first element is from the Gothic *und* ('up to' or 'before') and is cognate with the Latin *ante*. The basic idea behind this word is Old High German *zil* ('aim', 'point aimed at'; modern German *Ziel*), which with usage acquired a temporal as opposed to spatial meaning. In parts of northern England, however, 'I said till him' can still be heard, whereas 'I said to him' would be more normal in standard English.

b) The verb 'to till' is not totally unrelated to the preposition. Old English had the verb *tilian* ('to work at', 'to strive after', or 'to cultivate') and the agricultural associations did not appear until the thirteenth or fourteenth century. But the verb still retained much of its original meaning. When the ploughman 'tilled' the fields all day he was simultaneously 'striving' to grow the crops which would feed his family.

c) A little box where money is kept has been referred to as a 'till' since the seventeenth century, and its derivation owes much to the mechanism by which it is opened. Some boxes would have had a lid which was raised and lowered as and when necessary, but a 'till' had to be pulled or drawn open, hence its association with the Middle English verb *tillen* ('to draw'). In other words, the same idea lies behind the two nouns still in use today, 'till' and 'drawer'.

TOAST

Examples: a) He liked to sit by the fire and **toast** bread.
　　　　　 b) 'Let's raise a **toast** to the happy couple,' said Jim.

a) We now think of 'toasting' bread as presenting it to some source of heat until it is nicely browned and ready to be smothered with lashings of butter. The original meaning of the word, however, was simply to 'make dry' or 'to parch'. The word came into English in the fourteenth century as a borrowing from the Old French *toster*, itself a borrowing from the Latin *torrere* ('to dry up on account of the heat'). The relationship between the English and Latin words, however, is most clearly seen in the Latin participle *tostus* ('having been dried out'). Other cognates include 'terrain' (via the Latin noun *terra* ('dry land')) and 'torrid', the true meaning of which is 'dry and hot'. All of these expressions are close linguistic cousins of the word 'thirst', originally 'dryness' caused by the heat.

b) 'Drinking a toast' would appear at first to be something of a contradiction in terms as the availability of a drink cancels out the concept of thirst. The answer to the riddle is thought to lie in the publication of an article in eighteenth-century England. On 4 June 1709 the literary and society journal *The Tatler* (founded by Richard Steele and in circulation for only two years) published an article recounting how a young man in Bath, during the reign of Charles II (r. 1660–1685), established the custom of adding spiced toast to a drink in order to give it more flavour before raising it in honour of an attractive lady.

　　Whether or not this story is true we cannot be absolutely sure, but it is now considered the accepted explanation for the origin of the custom of 'raising a toast' or 'proposing a toast'. What we can be sure of, however, is that the English custom has found its way into several other European languages: French has *porter un toast à quelqu'un*; German has *einen Toast ausbringen*, and Russian has *predlozhit' tost*.

TOIL

Examples: a) They **toil** in the fields from dawn till dusk.

b) Nets, in a sporting context, are also known as **toils**.

a) The idea of 'toiling away' has come down to us by way of a very long path through social history. It has meant hard work in English since about 1300, but prior to that it signified disputes (frequently legal) and arguments. In Old French the verb *toeillier* meant 'to pull about', 'to drag around', and then, by extension, 'to make dirty'. It is not difficult to see the connection here with the Latin words from which the French verb is derived: *tudiculare* meant 'to smash using a *tudicula* or mill designed specifically for crushing olives'. *Tudicula* itself was derived from *tudes* ('hammer' or 'mallet'). A suitable parallel here would be the expression 'the daily grind', originating from the ancient labour-intensive custom of grinding corn in a quern.

b) By the sixteenth century English was using the word 'toil' to denote a net or nets used in hunting. This was a direct borrowing of the Old French *toile* ('linen cloth'), which had found its way into French from the Latin *tela* (surviving in modern Spanish with the same form and meaning), emphasizing the importance of weaving in the process of producing fabric. The Indo-European root here is **teks* ('to weave'), and other cognates include 'texture' and 'textile'.

At about the same time, French had acquired the derivative word *toilette* as a term for a bag, woven from cloth, in which clothes and personal items could be carried. By the 1680s the word had found its way into English, and 'toilet' was being used to define the act of dressing. An English lady of the day could be said to be 'at her toilet', with a piece of linen (or other form of 'textile') around her shoulders to prevent face powder falling on her dress.

In the early nineteenth century the word 'toilet' was being applied to the room in which a lady would dress and increasingly such a room would include sanitary ware. By 1895 this sanitary ware had become the most important feature of the room, causing a shift in meaning to what we understand by the word 'toilet' today.

TOLL

Examples: a) Motorway **tolls** in some countries can be quite high.

b) They **toll** the bells in the church every morning.

a) In Anglo-Saxon England a *toll* was a tax or rent that had to be paid on goods or property and was not used as a charge for the right to use a highway until the fifteenth century. It is cognate with the Old Norse *tollr*, Old High German *zol*, and modern German *Zoll*, all of which can trace their history back to medieval Latin *toloneum* ('toll house'). *Toloneum* was itself derived from the Greek *telōnion* ('customs house'), from *telos* ('a tax' or 'money that has to be paid to the state'). The primary meaning of *telos*, however, was 'end', 'completion', or 'fulfilment', the implication being that there was a certain finality concerning taxes due to the state; they were not subject to negotiation.

A comparison can be made here with our use of the word 'finance'. It is derived from the Old French verb *finer* ('to settle'; from the Latin *finis* ('end' or 'finish')) and was originally applied to the conclusion of business negotiations when payments had been agreed by all parties concerned. The word 'finance' was first applied to the management of (public) money in the eighteenth century.

Another fascinating linguistic association here is with the word 'philately'. This was a composite word devised in the nineteenth century to describe the new breed of aficionados, i.e., people who were passionate collectors of postage stamps. The word 'philately' combines the Greek *philein* ('to love') and *ateleia* ('articles not subject to payment'). The reference here is to the changes in the method of payment for receiving letters. It had been the custom for the recipient to pay for a letter received, but the advent of the postage stamp showed that payment had already been made and no further payment was to be demanded.

b) The origin of 'tolling' bells is not certain, but the most likely suggestion is that 'toll' in this sense is derived from an unrecorded Old English verb probably allied to *fortyllan*, meaning 'to lure' or 'to seduce'. We should assume that the former was intended here and that the church bells were 'tolled' in order to 'lure' or attract people to church for devotional purposes.

TRUNK

Examples: a) He had a large head and **trunk** but short arms.

b) She left home with a **trunk** containing all her belongings.

c) The elephant is recognizable by its **trunk**.

a) A man or woman's 'trunk' (i.e., the body stripped of arms, legs and the head) shares its linguistic derivation with the 'trunk' of a tree. Both are derived from the Latin verb *truncare* ('to shorten by cutting') extended in meaning to include the removal of any limbs, branches, etc., protruding from the main stock. Its derivative adjective *truncus* was used to describe almost anything that had been lopped, cut short, or even maimed.

Branches lopped off a tree, of course, can be fashioned into primitive clubs to be used as offensive or defensive weapons. Similar lengths of 'truncated' wood were used in the fourteenth century as shafts for spears and then, by the 1880s, the British police were being issued with specially polished versions known by another related word, 'truncheons'.

b) The relationship of *truncus* to a container is a little more difficult to explain. Old French had the word *tronc*, which in the twelfth century still meant the trunk of a tree or a wooden block. This then evolved somehow so that by the fifteenth century it meant an 'alms box' in a church. Possibly the original alms boxes were nothing more than lumps of wood hollowed out to form primitive containers. If this is indeed the origin, it would explain how *tronc* evolved over the centuries so that now it can refer to a large suit case or an American term for the storage compartment of a car known in British English as 'the boot'.

c) The elephant's proboscis has been referred to as a 'trunk' since the 1560s, and this is almost certainly due to confusion with the word 'trump', an archaic form of 'trumpet'. The word entered English in the early fourteenth century, derived from the Old French *trompe* (a long tubular musical instrument resembling the elephant's anatomical appendage), which had been around since the twelfth century. This word was cognate with the Italian *tromba* (the source of English 'trombone') but is thought to be of Old Norse origin.

The elephant's 'proboscis' is the Latin form of the Greek word *proboskis*. This comprises *pro-* ('in front') and *boskesthai* ('to graze') and thus literally means 'that which grazes in front'. And at the root of this verb we find *botanē*, Greek for 'grass' and the origin of the scientific term 'botany'.

USE

Examples: a) His wife has not learned how to **use** a computer yet.

              b) Larry **used** to go fishing but has lost interest now.

              c) He never buys new cars as he prefers **used** ones.

a) Latin had the infinitive *uti* ('to make use of', 'to practise', or 'to employ'), which is the derivation of such modern English words as 'utensil', 'utility', and 'utilize'. Etymologists have also posited the Vulgar Latin **usare* as a frequentative form of the same verb, with a past participle *usus* ('used'). The Old French derivative verb *user* ('to employ' or 'to practise') made its way into English in the early thirteenth century. By the late fourteenth century it had acquired the additional meaning of 'taking advantage of' a person or situation, not always for altruistic purposes.

b) The past tense of this verb can have two distinct meanings. It can simply replace the past of a verbal phrase such as 'to make use of' (e.g., 'I used a key to open the door.'), or it can express a repeated action in the past tense (e.g., 'She used to wake up every morning at six o'clock.'). This usage has been a feature of English since the thirteenth or fourteenth century and is derived from the intransitive verb (now no longer found) 'to use', which meant 'to practise regularly'.

c) In the world of commerce 'used' as a synonym for 'second-hand' is probably encountered most in the buying and selling of cars. We might be forgiven, therefore, for thinking that it is relatively modern interpretation of the word, but it has actually been a feature of the language since the 1590s.

VAN

Examples: a) He bought an old **van** for £500.

b) Amelia was in the **van** of modern authors.

a) We now tend to think of a 'van' as being a motor vehicle with no side windows and principally used for carrying goods, merchandise, etc. We also have the word 'caravan', which conveys a totally different idea, and yet the two words are connected in that the former is merely an abbreviated form of the latter. Nowadays, the word 'caravan' conjures up images of a mobile holiday home towed behind a car, but the original caravans were something quite different. The word came into English via Old French *caravane* (a direct borrowing from the Persian *kārwān*), the term used to denote a line of camels making slow and arduous progress across the desert. There is also the very plausible suggestion that the word is ultimately derived from the Sanskrit *karabhah* ('camel').

In the sixteenth century 'caravan' was applied to a line of ships, and by the seventeenth century it had acquired the meaning of a 'covered wagon', usually pulled behind a moving column and containing food and stores. This explains the association with the modern concept of it as a vehicle used for the transport of goods. And the last carriage on a train, usually referred to as the 'guard's van', is the compartment where the guard sits and bulky goods can be stored during transit.

b) A 'guard's van', however, has nothing whatever to do with a 'vanguard' which was originally a military term. In Middle English it was referred to as the *vantguard*, an adapted form of the Old French *avant-garde* ('forward protection'). As its name suggests, in any military encounter its task was to position itself ahead of and protect the main body of an advancing army.

The expression 'in the van' is an abbreviation of 'in the vanguard' and has now widened its meaning to include activities other than those of a purely military nature. Anyone so described would now be considered as leading the way or, to use a particularly modern expression, 'at the cutting edge' of a movement or social trend. A more established phrase for the same concept is, of course, 'avant-garde'.

VICE

Examples: a) The officer was transferred to the **Vice** Squad.

b) The carpenter caught his thumb in a **vice**.

c) The **vice** president was late for the meeting.

a) The Latin word from which 'vice' in this sense is derived is *vitium* ('physical defect' or 'fault'). The Romans also applied the word figuratively to behaviour when identifying moral weakness, deficiency, and even criminal tendencies. The word entered English via French in the twelfth or thirteenth century.

The term 'vice squad' was coined in the United States in 1905 to designate the branch of the police force tasked with chasing criminals involved in drugs, illegal gambling, and prostitution.

The derivative adjective 'vicious' originally meant 'associated with crime' and acquired its present association with violent aggressiveness in the early eighteenth century. The term 'vicious circle', suggesting a difficult or unpleasant situation with no apparent way out, dates from around 1840.

b) In the fourteenth century *vice* was an Anglo-French term for a winch or crane which would have been operated by some sort of 'winding' mechanism. This is also the basic concept behind the modern workshop tool operated by a screw being turned until a length of wood or metal can be held in a firm, 'vice-like' grip.

c) 'Vice' as a term for a substitute is derived from the Latin *vice* ('in place of'), the ablative case of an unrecorded noun *vix* with the genitive case *vicis*. The Latin expression always suggests change, interchange, or substitution and is itself cognate with the Greek *eikein* (from an earlier root *wik-*) 'to yield' and hence 'to submit' or 'to obey'. The implication here is that anybody whose position or role is defined by the prefix is always subordinate to a higher authority.

The expression 'vice versa', dating from around 1600, is the ablative of *vix/vicis* ('change') plus the feminine past participle of *vertere* ('to turn'), meaning 'the order of things having been changed'.

Another derivative noun in English is 'vicar' (from the Latin adjective *vicarius* ('substitute')), the church official who traditionally answered to a rector.

Ultimately, the word 'vice' is linguistically related to the word 'weak' and even the 'wych elm', so called because its branches droop and appear to lack vigour.

WAGE

Examples: a) The workers always collected their **wages** on Friday night.

b) Countries frequently **wage** war on their neighbours.

a) In Middle English the noun *wage* was the term for anything offered as a pledge or deposit. It was related to the Old Norman French *wagier* and Old French *gagier* meaning 'to pledge', 'to promise', as well as 'to bet'. This explains how in modern English the noun 'wage' means 'money earned', but its derivative verb, 'to wager', is a synonym for 'to place a bet'.

The use of the word in English to define payment for work completed dates from the fourteenth century, and the concept of a 'pledge' is retained today, even if the fact is not always appreciated. The worker 'pledges' to work in return for an agreed amount of money, and the employer 'pledges' to pay for work done.

The French words *wagier* and *gagier* were both derived from the Low Latin *wadium* which in turn is thought to be a borrowing from a Germanic source. Gothic, for instance, had *wadi* 'to pledge', closely connected to Old English *wedd* (a pledge or agreement) and its modern derivative verb 'to wed'. Weddings are, after all, ceremonies involving two people who exchange vows or 'pledges'.

b) The expression 'to wage war' is simply a derivative of the above. The original idea was not the actual engagement in acts of war but merely the 'pledge' to do so.

In the thirteenth century the term for a man who 'pledged' to fight for his lord and master was *souldeour*, from the Old French *saudier*. This was a term dating back to Roman times when a fighting man was rewarded for his service by payment in gold coins known in Latin as *solidi* (singular *solidus*). The word survives in modern English 'soldier'.

Sometimes, however, Roman soldiers were paid a *salarium*, an allowance with which they were expected to buy salt (*sal* in Latin). This is the origin of the modern English 'salary'.

WAKE

Examples: a) The ship's **wake** could be seen for miles.

b) '**Wake** me at 7:30, please,' said the hotel guest.

c) After the funeral they all attended the **wake**.

a) It will probably come as no surprise, but the trail left in the water behind a ship, the wake, is historically linked to a word meaning wet. To find the explanation for this apparent oddity we have to consider the Scandinavian origins of the word. It was first applied to the trail behind a moving vessel in the 1540s, but its origin is the Old Norse *vök* ('hole in the ice') and the adjective *vökr* ('damp'). If we imagine how dry the snow and ice can be in the northern climes, we can also understand how 'wet' the water would have appeared once a hole had been broken through the ice.

b) The verb 'to wake' or 'waken' has come down to us from two very similar Old English verbs, *wacan* ('to become awake') and *wacian* ('to be or remain awake'). These are cognate with Old Norse *vaka* and modern German *wachen* ('to be awake'). The Indo-European root here is **weg* ('to be strong' or 'to be lively'), which is also the derivation of the Latin verb *vigere* ('to be strong') and the adjective *vigil* ('watchful' or 'alert'). The same root and Latin derivatives provided English with words such as 'vigour', 'vigilante', and 'vigilant'. Also, strange as it may seem, it is the derivation of the word 'vegetable' (something that grows 'vigorously'). By contrast, the English word 'sleep' is cognate with the German verb *schlafen* and the related adjective *schlaff* ('limp', 'slack', or 'lifeless').

c) The custom of sitting up all night with a corpse (i.e., keeping vigil) dates from the fifteenth century and although the custom has more or less died out in Western cultures, there is a surviving linguistic relic. The 'wake', which can often develop into a rowdy party in honour of the dear departed, has its origins in the practice of keeping watch over the body the night before the burial.

Until relatively recently, mill and factory workers in the north of England traditionally had two weeks' holiday in the summer known as 'wakes weeks'. Originally these holidays had been associated with church services held late in the evening and continuing through the night, obliging worshippers to 'stay awake'. But during the industrial revolution these holidays acquired a progressively more secular significance.

WAX

Examples: a) **Wax** is good for protecting wood and furniture.
b) He began to **wax** eloquent about his pupil.

a) Wax now can be produced from so many substances and chemicals that we tend to forget that the original wax was the sticky substance secreted by bees. In Old English the term for this substance was *weax*, and this is thought to be cognate with the Old High German *waba* ('honeycomb') and derived from the Indo-European root **weg* or **wab* ('to weave'). The connection here is explained by the primitive belief that bees wove their honeycombs much in the same way that spiders construct webs. The linguistic result is that modern English words such as 'wax', 'web', and 'weave' are all cognate.

b) When we talk about a speaker who 'waxes eloquent' or a 'waxing' (as opposed to waning) moon we are using a word derived from a very different source, despite the similarity of form.

In this sense, 'to wax' is a rather archaic verb meaning 'to grow' or 'to increase' and survives now only in set phrases or poetry. It is a relative of the modern German *wachsen*, the normal verb for 'to grow', and is closely connected to verbs with the same meaning in other European languages such as Swedish *växa* and Danish *vokse*.

But the story does not end there. If we travel even further back in time we find that this word is related to the Indo-European root *weg* ('to be strong'). The same root produced the ancient Greek and Latin verbs *auxein* and *augere*, which both meant 'to grow', 'to increase', or 'to prosper'. These verbs went on to give us words such as 'to augment' and even 'auction', which, after all, is simply a selling technique that involves a progressively 'increasing' cost to the buyer.

WEIGH

Examples: a) She liked to **weigh** herself every morning.

b) The captain gave the order to **weigh** anchor.

a) In modern English the literal meaning of the verb 'to weigh' usually involves a process of assessing how heavy something is. But it was not always so. Originally the verb was always associated with movement, as is clear when we look at its linguistic history and consider some of its modern cognate expressions. The Indo-European root from which it is derived was *wegh* meaning 'to move'. The same root produced Sanskrit *vahati* ('it moves') and the Latin *vehere* 'to convey' which gave English the word 'vehicle'. Other close linguistic relatives include 'wagon' and the same word in a slightly different form 'wain'. And, to reinforce the association with travel or motion, we should also mention that 'way' (a track or path along which wagons move) is yet another direct linguistic relative.

The development in meaning from movement to heaviness is not difficult to understand. If wagons, wains, etc., had to be loaded with goods before they could be conveyed to their destination, the people tasked with the job would have soon realized that loading carts frequently involved moving heavy boxes, goods, and materials. And lifting large or bulky objects soon fostered an appreciation of weight.

b) An archaic nautical expression which has survived to the modern day, of course, is 'to weigh anchor'. This has nothing to do with putting the anchor on a pair of scales; it simply preserves the original idea of lifting or moving a heavy object and loading it onto the deck before a ship can sail.

In the fourteenth century 'to weigh' acquired an additional, figurative usage of 'considering the possibilities' as in such modern phrases as 'weighing up one's options'.

WELL

Examples: a) He sang rather **well**.

b) The **well** was very deep.

c) '**Well**!' said the teacher, displaying his astonishment.

a) We now think of 'well' as the adverb of the adjective 'good'. And the word 'goodly', which looks like an adverb but is an adjective, has always been synonymous with 'handsome' and 'good looking'. Old English and Middle English both had *wel*, Old Norse had *vel*, and Old High German had *wela*, all of which meant the same as the modern English adverb 'well'. Curiously, however, all were derived from the Indo-European root **wel/*wol* ('to be pleasing'), the same root that provided the word 'will', an alternative to 'wish'. This means that the original sense of 'well' was 'according to one's wishes', so that if we say that someone sings rather 'well', what we mean historically is that his or her singing is as we would 'will' or 'wish' it to be.

In the thirteenth century 'well' was synonymous with 'happy' or 'fortunate', and since the middle of the sixteenth it has implied good health.

b) Historically, 'well' as a noun did not refer to the shaft down which a bucket was lowered when water was needed on the surface; it referred to the water itself. Most, if not all, of the Germanic languages have the word in one form or another but with slightly different meanings: Old English and Middle English had *welle* ('spring' or 'fountain'; from *wellen* ('to bubble' or 'boil up')); Old High German had *wella* ('wave'), and Old Norse had *vella* ('raging torrent'). Modern Russian has the cognate *volna* as the normal word for a 'wave'.

All of these variants are allied to the Latin *volvere* ('to turn') and the Old High German verb *waltzen* ('to spin' or 'to revolve'), the verb which also produced the modern ballroom dance known throughout the world as 'the waltz'.

c) It is difficult to explain the use of 'well' as an interjection or expression of surprise with any certainty of conviction. All we can confidently state is that it was used as far back as Anglo-Saxon times as it is found in Old English.

WORRY

Examples: a) Pete began to **worry** about paying off his debts.
               b) Farmers shoot dogs that **worry** their sheep.

a) It was not until relatively recently that the verb 'to worry' was applied to troubled minds. Its intransitive use (e.g., 'he worries about . . .') has been in common use only since about 1860 and its transitive use (e.g., 'don't let it worry you') since the 1820s. The word acquired the meaning 'to annoy' at some time in the seventeenth century, but the original use of the word was far more physical. The Indo-European root from which it is derived is **werg* ('to bend' or 'to twist'), found in the Old English *wyrgan* ('to choke', 'to strangle', or 'to tear'). The linguistic development from physical strangulation to psychological disturbance has a parallel in Greek where the verb *agkhein* ('to throttle' or 'to press tight') produced words in English such as the medical condition 'angina' (a heart condition producing feelings of tightness in the chest) and the psychological states 'anger', 'anguish', and 'anxiety'. By contrast, when Russian speakers use the term *angina,* they are using the word in a way which arguably remains closer to the original sense of the Indo-European root. It is the Russian term for 'tonsillitis', a condition characterized by the patient's difficulty in swallowing.

In addition to providing the origin of the verb 'to worry', the Indo-European root **werg* also produced the Latin verb *vergere* ('to bend') and the English noun 'verge'. This word is now used mainly to define the area where the surrounding land slopes or 'bends' down to the roadway, but it also has another interesting usage. A 'verge' was traditionally a flexible (i.e., 'bendable') rod carried as a staff of office by certain church officials. And they are known as 'vergers'.

b) Nowadays, when a farmer shoots a dog because it has been 'worrying' his sheep he is probably using the modern meaning of the word (i.e., 'causing mental anguish'). His historical counterpart, however, would have meant something far more dramatic by the term. In Anglo-Saxon England the verb *wyrgan* meant specifically 'to choke', and then by the fourteenth century it had come to mean specifically 'seize by the throat with the teeth'.

YARD

Examples: a) Pete always leaves his bike in the **yard**.
　　　　　 b) There are three feet in one **yard**.

a) This is an ancient word with more than a few linguistic relatives not only in English but also in many European languages. The Indo-European root **ghorto* meant 'to grasp' and, by extension, 'to enclose', and virtually all of the cognate descendants preserve this concept. Old English had *geard* (where the 'g' would have been pronounced as a modern 'y') for 'enclosure', Latin had *hortus* for 'garden' (the derivation of the English word 'horticulture'), Russian has *gorod* for 'town', Irish has *gort* for 'field', and ancient Greek had *khortos*, which was used to designate an enclosed area specifically set aside for feeding cattle, etc. It is also the origin of the English noun 'court' in all its meanings.

The word 'orchard' may not look at first sight as though it is linguistically related to 'yard', but it is. The Old English term was *ortgeard*, which was a contraction of an earlier *wortgeard* (also *wyrtgeard*) where *wort* (or *wyrt*) meant 'vegetable' or 'fruit', giving the literal meaning as 'fruit or vegetable yard or garden'.

b) As a unit of measurement, the 'yard' has fallen somewhat out of usage in modern English and has largely been replaced by the metre. But it has not disappeared altogether and survives in expressions such as 'the whole nine yards', 'a yard of ale', and 'give him an inch and he will take a yard'.

The Old English *gerd* meant a 'stick' or 'pole' (Dutch still has *gard* for a 'twig' or 'rod'), and was also used as a measuring device. In Anglo-Saxon times a 'yard' was a linear unit of land measurement thought to have equated to about five metres in modern terminology. It shortened considerably in the fourteenth century to thirty-six inches, a definition that still stands today.

The 'yard', of course, is divided into three feet and each foot consists of twelve inches. The use of 'foot' as a unit of measurement is self-explanatory, but the 'inch' has an interesting history. It is derived from the Latin *uncia* which was used to define the twelfth part of any whole and is consequently also the origin of the English unit of troy weight, the 'ounce'.

ZEST

Examples: a) This recipe requires the **zest** of three lemons.

b) He was depressed and lost his **zest** for life.

a) Since the 1670s the word 'zest' in a culinary context has referred almost exclusively to the top layer of peel on an orange or lemon, pared off in extremely thin slices and added to a dish for extra flavour or piquancy. In Middle French, however, it was the term applied to the thick membrane dividing the kernel of a walnut. The word is thought to be a borrowing from Latin *scindere* ('to split') and the Greek *skhistos* ('divided'), from the verb *skhizein* ('to split' or 'to cleave'). If this is the correct etymology of the word, it makes it cognate with other nouns dealing with separation, division, and cutting such as 'scissors', 'scythe', 'schism', and the prefix 'schizo-' in terms such as 'schizophrenia' (a divided mind) and 'schizoid' (possessing characteristics resembling those of a schizophrenic mind).

b) There is no definitive explanation for the word 'zest' being used as a synonym for 'enthusiasm' or 'eagerness'. It has, however, been used in this way since around 1790, and the most likely derivation of the usage is the sharpness associated with a slice of a citrus fruit being compared to a person's character. A man or woman described as having a 'zest' for living is likely to be characterized by a certain sharpness and a distinctive personality. Much the same could be said about a slice of lemon.

Glossary of Terms

Ablative case. The form of the noun or pronoun indicating an agent, instrument, or location (e.g., the dog was shot *by the farmer*; he was *away from home*).

Accusative case. The form of a noun or pronoun when it is the object of a verb (e.g., I saw *them*).

Albanian. Spoken in Albania, it constitutes a separate branch of the Indo-European group.

Basque. A language spoken in the area straddling the border between southern France and northern Spain. It is known officially as a 'language isolate' because it displays no known links with any other language. It is generally recognized as being older than the Indo-European family group.

Celtic. An Indo-European group of languages which includes Breton, Cornish, Welsh, Manx, Scots Gaelic, and Irish Gaelic.

Cognate. If a word is described as being 'cognate' with another, it does not mean that one was derived from the other but that they both are descended from a common ancestor. For example, the English 'brother', the German *Bruder*, and the Gothic *brothar* are all cognate because their shared origin is the Sanskrit *bhratri*.

Coptic. Now surviving only as the liturgical language of the Coptic Church, Coptic is usually described as representing the final stages in the development of ancient Egyptian.

Dative case. The form of the noun or pronoun when it is the indirect object, i.e., that something is being done *to* someone or something (e.g., I gave the book *to the boy*).

Dravidian. Non-Indo-European group of languages spoken mainly in southern India.

East Frisian. A dialect of German spoken mainly in an area straddling the border between modern Germany and the Netherlands.

Genitive case. The form of a noun or pronoun when used to indicate possession (e.g., *the boy's* coat was lying on the floor).

Gothic. A reasonably well-documented East Germanic language; the oldest known documents date from the fourth century AD. The language was more or less extinct by the eighth or ninth century.

Greek. Dating back to the third millennium BC, Greek is the world's oldest recorded living language.

Hindi. A language of northern India belonging to the Indo-European group. Closely related to Urdu, it is the official language of India.

Hungarian. Although surrounded by Indo-European languages because of its position in central Europe, Hungarian belongs to the Finno-Ugric group. It is closely related to Finnish and Estonian.

Infinitive. The part of the verb from which all other parts are derived. In English, it is usually identified by the word 'to' as in 'to live', 'to have', 'to be', etc.

Late Latin. Latin as spoken and written approximately between the third and sixth centuries AD.

Latin. Normally refers to what is also known as classical Latin, the language of ancient Rome from 75 BC to the third century AD.

Medieval Latin. Latin used throughout Europe as the language of scholarly communication in the world of administration, science, literature, and the law between the fifth and fifteenth centuries.

Middle English. The language of Chaucer, Gower, etc. Dating from the beginning of the twelfth century to the middle of the fifteenth century, it is probably best described as late Old English strongly influenced by Norman French.

Middle French. A later stage of Old French, Middle French flourished in Europe from the fourteenth century until c. 1610.

Middle High German. Spoken in southern Germany and extended into Austria and Switzerland AD 1050–1350, although some authorities consider that it lasted until 1500.

Nominative case. The form of noun or pronoun expressing the subject of a verb (e.g., *the man* bought a new car).

Oblique case. Any grammatical case other than the nominative or vocative.

Old Church Slavonic. First Slavonic (or Slavic) literary language. An Indo-European language spoken in Eastern Europe around the ninth century AD.

Old English. Now the preferred term for what was formerly known as Anglo-Saxon. Related to Icelandic, German, and the Scandinavian languages, it was spoken in most of England between the mid-fifth century and the mid-twelfth century.

Old French. A Romance language spoken in Europe from the ninth to the fourteenth century.

Old High German. The earliest stage in the development of German, dating from c. AD 700–1050.

Old Norse. Northern Germanic language spoken mainly in Scandinavia from the eighth to the fourteenth century AD.

Old Persian. An Indo-European language dating from 525–300 BC, and spoken in an area now covered by Iran, Iraq, Turkey, and Egypt.

Old Prussian. An extinct language once spoken in what is now part of northern Poland and Russian-administered Kaliningrad.

Phoenician. An ancient Semitic language spoken in an area covered largely by modern Lebanon and Syria.

Proto-Germanic. Reconstructed parent language of all Germanic and Scandinavian languages and dating from c. 500 BC.

Provençal. A variety of French spoken mainly in the far south of France, but also extends into Italy and Monaco. Traditionally, the language of the medieval troubadours.

Romance languages. The family of European languages descended from Latin. The main languages in this group are: French, Spanish, Portuguese, Romanian, and Italian.

Romany. An Indo-European language spoken by the Romany (or Gypsy) people. First attested in Europe in the sixteenth century.

Sanskrit. One of the oldest known Indo-European languages. A scholarly language considered sacred to Hinduism and dating back as far as the second millennium BC.

Slavonic languages. Eastern branch of the Indo-European group which includes Russian, Bulgarian, Polish, Czech, and Ukrainian.

Umbrian. The language of ancient Umbria in central Italy, related to Latin.

Vocative case. The form of a noun or pronoun when being addressed or spoken to (e.g., *Tom*, come here!).

Vulgar Latin. The vernacular or colloquial language spoken by the general populace throughout the Roman Empire and from which the Romance languages developed between the sixth and ninth centuries AD.

Bibliography

Atherton, Mark. *Old English*. Teach Yourself Series. London: Hodder Education, 2006.

Atkins, Beryl T., Alain Duval, and Rosemary C. Milne. *Collins-Robert French Dictionary*. Paris: Harper Collins, 1992.

Ayto, John. *Dictionary of Word Origins*. London: Bloomsbury, 1990.

Barber, Charles L. *The Story of Language*. London: Pan Books, 1964.

Barney, Stephen A. *Word-Hoard: An Introduction to Old English Vocabulary*. London: Yale University Press, 1977.

Chernykh, P. Ya. *Istoriko-etimologicheskiy slovar' russkogo yazyka* [Historical etymological dictionary of the Russian language]. Moscow: Russkiy yazyk, 2001.

Crystal, David. *The Cambridge Encyclopedia of Language*. Cambridge: Cambridge University Press, 1987.

———. *The Cambridge Encyclopedia of the English Language*. Cambridge: Cambridge University Press, 1995.

Dinneen, Patrick S. *Foclóir Gaedhilge agus Béarla* [An Irish-English dictionary]. Dublin: Educational Company of Ireland, 1965.

Falla, Paul, Marcus Wheeler, and Boris Unbegaun. *The Oxford Russian Dictionary*. Oxford: Oxford University Press, 1993.

Hawkins, Joyce M. *The Oxford Reference Dictionary*. London: Guild Publishing, 1991.

Hoad, T. F., ed. *The Concise Dictionary of English Etymology*. Oxford: Oxford University Press, 1996.

Jarman, Beatriz Galimberti, and Roy Russell. *The Oxford Spanish Dictionary*. Oxford: Oxford University Press, 1994.

Lewis, Henry. *Collins-Spurrell Welsh Dictionary*. London: Collins, 1962.

Liddell, Henry George, and Robert Scott. *Greek-English Lexicon*. Oxford: Clarendon Press, 1963 [1864].

Maclennan, Malcolm. *A Pronouncing and Etymological Dictionary of the Gaelic Language*. Aberdeen: Acair and Aberdeen University Press, 1979.

McArthur, Tom. *The Oxford Companion to the English Language*. Oxford: Oxford University Press, 1992.

Shipley, Joseph T. *The Origins of English Words*. Baltimore: Johns Hopkins University Press, 1984.

Simpson, D. P. *Cassell's New Latin-English English-Latin Dictionary*. London: Cassell, 1959.

Skeat, Walter W. *The Concise Dictionary of English Etymology*. Wordsworth Reference. Hertfordshire: Ware, 1993.

———. *An Etymological Dictionary of the English Language*. Oxford: Clarendon Press, 1974.

Terrell, Peter, Calderwood-Schnorr, Veronika, Wendy V. A. Morris, and Roland Breitsprecher. *Collins German-English English-German Dictionary*. Oxford: Oxford University Press, 1990.

Thompson, Della, ed. *The Concise Oxford Dictionary*. 9th ed. London: Oxford University Press, 1995.

Wade, Terence. *Russian Etymological Dictionary*. London: Bristol Classical Press, 1996.

Wyld, Henry Cecil, ed. *The Universal Dictionary of the English Language*. London: Waverley, 1956.

On-line sources

Arthur, Ross G. *English–Old Norse Dictionary*. Linguistics Series, Cambridge, Ontario: Parentheses Publications, 2002. http://www.yorku.ca/inpar/language/English-Old_Norse.pdf.

Clark Hall, John R. *A Concise Anglo-Saxon Dictionary*. 2nd ed. New York: Macmillan, 1916. http://www.ling.upenn.edu/~kurisuto/germanic/oe_clarkhall_about.html.

Harper, Douglas. *Online Etymological Dictionary*. 2001–. http://www.etymonline.com/bio.php.

Linguistics Research Center. University of Texas at Austin. http://www.utexas.edu/cola/centers/lrc/.

Sweet, Henry. *The Student's Dictionary of Anglo-Saxon*. Oxford: Clarendon Press, 1897. https://archive.org/details/studentsdictiona00sweerich.

MyEtymology.com

Wikipedia: The Free Encyclopedia. San Francisco: Wikimedia Foundation. http://en.wikipedia.org/.